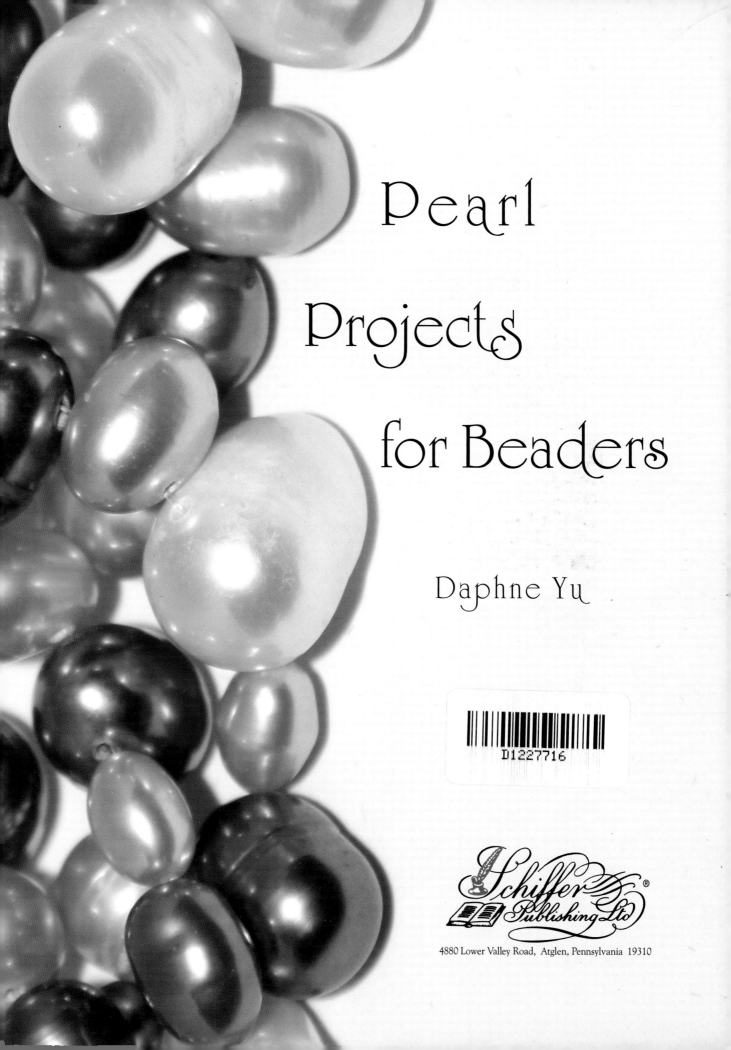

Pearl

Projects

for Beaders

Daphne Yu

Schiffer Publishing Ltd®

4880 Lower Valley Road, Atglen, Pennsylvania 19310

Dedication

I dedicate this book to my parents. They taught me that an attractive appearance is of no value and what is underneath is the only thing that matters. Substance and content are long lasting and much more valuable. I have applied this to my designs. They cannot look pretty just for a few days; they not only have to last, but also provide a comfortable wear. My parents have always encouraged me to excel, making me believe that hard work will eventually pay off.

My sister and two brothers are also excellent role models, and I am proud to be able to follow their example.

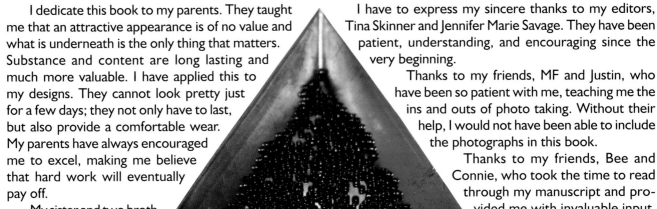

Acknowledgments

I have to express my sincere thanks to my editors, Tina Skinner and Jennifer Marie Savage. They have been patient, understanding, and encouraging since the very beginning.

Thanks to my friends, MF and Justin, who have been so patient with me, teaching me the ins and outs of photo taking. Without their help, I would not have been able to include the photographs in this book.

Thanks to my friends, Bee and Connie, who took the time to read through my manuscript and provided me with invaluable input. Lastly, I have to thank my son, Austin, for helping me with the computer and the photography.

Other Schiffer Books on Related Subjects:

Bead Crochet Jewelry: Tools, Tips, and 15 Beautiful Projects,
0-7643-2023-8, $18.95

Beads & Agate Jewelry to Create Yourself,
978-0-7643-2998-2, $14.99

Charts on pages 97-99, courtesy of and copyright by Swarovski AG:

CREATE YOUR STYLE with SWAROVSKI ELEMENTS

Designed by Stephanie Daugherty
Type set in University Roman LET/University Roman Alts LET/ Humanst521 BT
ISBN: 978-0-7643-3552-5
Printed in China

Schiffer Books are available at special discounts for bulk purchases for sales promotions or premiums. Special editions, including personalized covers, corporate imprints, and excerpts can be created in large quantities for special needs. For more information contact the publisher:

Schiffer Publishing Ltd.
4880 Lower Valley Road
Atglen, PA 19310
Phone: (610) 593-1777;
Fax: (610) 593-2002
E-mail: Info@schifferbooks.com

For the largest selection of fine reference books on this and related subjects, please visit our web site at:

www.schifferbooks.com

We are always looking for people to write books on new and related subjects. If you have an idea for a book please contact us at the above address.

This book may be purchased from the publisher.
Include $5.00 for shipping.
Please try your bookstore first.
You may write for a free catalog.

In Europe, Schiffer books are distributed by
Bushwood Books
6 Marksbury Ave.
Kew Gardens
Surrey TW9 4JF England
Phone: 44 (0) 20 8392 8585; Fax: 44 (0) 20 8392 9876
E-mail: info@bushwoodbooks.co.uk
Website: www.bushwoodbooks.co.uk

Contents

Be Inspired

Be Inspired

Beads are colorful and attractive whereas pearls are unique in color, luster, shape, and size. Every woman loves to have a strand of pearls in her jewelry collection. There are a variety of pearl projects here: pearls mixed with crystals; pearls on their own, and pearls together with other semi-precious stones. They are fun and easy-to-make; you will definitely find something that you like in this book.

When it comes to beading, experience is the key. After you have done a number of projects, you will improve and, very soon, you will be finishing piece after piece in no time. If you don't have many friends now, you will — as you will enjoy sharing your creations with them.

I love pearls. I have been fascinated with pearls for as long as I can remember. My mom's pearl necklace lay broken in a tin box for the longest time. I wondered why she did not have it fixed. Those pearls were not very big, but they were round and shiny. They had that rainbow-like shine that would fascinate any little girl. I cannot restring that necklace for her now. However, I made one gray pearl necklace with a pearl pendant and presented it to her as a gift about two years ago. She did not say much at the time, but I have noticed she has worn it on many different occasions since. There is this satisfaction that I experience when I see people wearing my creations — and this experience with my mom was really special.

When I started my first job, my first piece of jewelry was also a strand of pearls. I still remember I brought it from Sears, and I had worn it on many special occasions. The strand is of cultured salt-water pearls. The shine is different from the shine on a strand of fresh water pearls. There is a big difference in price between salt-water pearls and fresh water pearls. The best way to judge the quality of either pearl is to place them on a medium-gray color surface and view them under diffused natural daylight.

I used mostly fresh water pearls and some crystal pearls for the projects in this book. Pearls are so versatile that you can do many different things with them. I hope I have included the ones that would interest you. For fresh

Mix of fresh water pearls.

water pearls, there are many grades. They come in different colors, shapes, and sizes. You can easily find something that fascinates you and agrees with your budget. I have included some of the more common and readily available ones here. There are projects on necklaces, bracelets, watches, earrings, and rings. Shall we begin?

I hope you enjoy what I have put together for you. Just look around you for ideas, colors, shapes, and pattern combinations. I have learned a lot since I started working with beads. There is always more to learn and even more to try out. If you would like to give me comments on the book, please write me at info@aikm.net. If you are a novice beader and would like to refresh on some beading techniques, you can read through *Section Two* first. Otherwise, skip to any projects that you like.

Finding Inspiration

I take inspirations from my surroundings. Places have their unique colors. When you see a scenic photo of a place, you can feel the atmosphere, the temperature, and the scent. I have lived in three very different places at different stages of my life and enjoyed them all; they are all different in their unique ways. The color here in Singapore is very different from the East Coast of the United States. It is also different from my birthplace, Hong Kong. Keep your eyes and mind open. The inspirations will come to you naturally and gently.

You can even be inspired by music. When you hear a piece of music, you get an image in your mind. It can be bold, heavy, colorful, and hot — just like Singapore's weather. The rain can be heavy here. The raindrops on the window are big and streaks of water flow down fast and furious. The snow melting on the windscreen of a car is so rhythmic and yet random. Feel, listen, and pay attention to the details and observe the difference. Listen to the whisper of the rain or the snow. Smell the fresh air, feel the breeze…Open your eyes and mind to what nature is telling you. The different seasons give you very different color schemes. The amber and golden hues of autumn, mixed

A mixture of gold and beige.

Violet haze — A mixture of off white large quartz chips, tourmaline chips, purple velvet crystal beads, and hematite stars.

Turquoise color donut and turquoise color chips are mixed with silver-colored spacers, blue zircon crystal beads, and glass beads.

The combination of black, silver, and red creates a strong contrast.

This blue mix is comprised of Chinese ceramic beads and Indian glass beads.

All natural earthy color with just wood and shell beads.

with a bit of brown and green, is a profusion of colors that is bold yet calming to the nerve. The silvery white glitter of icicles on the wiry gray tree branches remind me of this magical scene of a quiet fantasyland.

You can also be inspired by ordinary every day events. For example, when you visit the market, look at the colorful fruits and vegetables. It is amazing, all these beautiful colors: the shiny purple eggplants next to the bright orange carrots. Isn't that a great color combination? If it is too bold for you, use big purple beads and place a small orange crystal in between. If it is still too daring, try adding neutral colors like white, clear, and black to tone it down.

When you are making your own designs, color is the most important. There is no hard and fast rule on what is good or bad. See the color combinations in the accom-panying photos? Harmonize the color and the size and shape will come naturally. Notice what is pretty around you. It can be a painting, a handbag, or even a bird. Pay attention to the color combinations and design... How does it make you feel? You can incorporate them all into your creations.

Place your favorite beads in a transparent container and watch them mingle together. Very often a new com-bination will come to mind — something that you had not visualized before. Trendy materials are all around you; the color on the web, the commercials on TV, the billboard signs that stare at you every morning as you drive pass. Subconsciously, you're taking in all these things and they're influencing you and, when you see something beautifully breath-taking, you will be able to recognize it.

Good Practice

When you are inspired, you will want to do a lot of beading. Here are some practical tips for you to keep in mind before you start.

- Have a clean workspace, a good chair, and enough light to work with. Rest your eyes and fingers from time to time.

- Always wash your hands before and after beading.

- When cutting or trimming wires, always place the wire and cutter at a safe distance from your eyes and other people.

- Measure the length of the string on your neck or wrist to save time. Allow six inches on each side for knot-ting on a necklace.

- Start a piece from the center. This way when you are short on focal beads, you can fill the sides with matching spacers to make a great piece.

- When working on a piece, check the piece in front of a mirror to see how it looks on you. This is the only way you can be certain that the length suits you. At the same time, you can feel the weight of the beads and see if they sit comfortably around your neck.

- Keep the beads, findings, and tools in good order, so you can locate the items that you need.

- For silver or silver-colored findings, it is good to keep them away from moisture by keeping them in sealed cellophane plastics. Resealable plastic bags like Ziploc™ cannot keep moisture out.

- When not working on a piece, you can use stationary clips to secure the loose strands. Place it in a Zi-ploc™ bag until you can finish it.

- When doing a weave design using multiple nylon strings — for example in a case of a three-nylon strand design — you can hold all three nylon strands in your hand. Arrange the ends as long, longer, and longest, and always bead the longest one first. This way, you will know which strand you are working on at all times.

- You can use seed beads and spacers when you are a few beads short.

- Place less chunky beads on the side of the neck for more comfortable wear.

- For findings, there are many different colors, includ-ing silver, gold, brass, and dark tone. You will want to have the findings in the correct color to match your beads; all findings should be in matching color within the set.

- Different beads have different hole sizes. When do-ing a necklace with leather or faux suede, try the beads out on the stringing materials first. If the hole size of the bead is too large, you can cover it with a bead cap or put a spacer next to it to hide the gaping hole.

1

The Projects

Cicely

Materials

Necklace
- **1** plus strand 84 pieces 0.20" (5mm) gray pearls
- **1** 1.02" (26mm) silver flower
- **6** 0.47" (12mm) silver flowers
- **1** 30" (76cm) nylon string
- **2** clamshell bead tips
- **2** crimps
- **2** jump rings
- **1** clasp

Earrings
- **8** 0.20" (5mm) gray pearls
- **2** 0.47" (12mm) silver flowers
- **2** strands 3" (8cm) silver-colored wire, 26 gauge thickness
- **1** set of earring wires

Three simple items for this Cicely necklace and earrings set.

Cicely

What to Do

Take the nylon and start beading from the center. Insert the large silver flower and then string six pearls on either side of the flower. Add one little flower, then five pearls, and another little flower. Follow this pattern and, when you have three little flowers on each side of the main silver flower, you are done with the pattern.

Continue adding gray pearls until you reach the desired length. End with a clamshell bead tip. Secure it with the crimp bead and bring the string back through the beads and proceed with the standard ending procedure (see Section Two: Basic Skills). If you are right-handed, put the lobster clasp on the right side of the necklace so that you can hold the lobster claw with your right hand for easy manipulation. If you are left-handed, do the opposite. As this Cicely motif has a front and back, you need to make sure the clasp is placed correctly. (We have a button clasp in this sample; put the flower on the left, and the clip on the right.)

Start from the middle and complete the motif first.

Earrings

Repeat the same procedure for the second earring. Check to make sure the two earrings match.

Use silver-colored wire for the earrings. Follow the pattern in the picture. Put one flower in between the pearls and then make the loop to attach to the earring wire using your round-nose pliers.

Bold

Materials

Necklace

- **14** 0.39" (10mm) oblong pearls
- **9** 0.31" (8mm) SWAROVSKI® ELEMENTS Bead Art 5301
- **6** 0.31" (8mm) SWAROVSKI® ELEMENTS Art 5000
- **18** brownish gold seed beads 11/0 size
- **18** 0.08" (2mm) gold-colored beads
- **28** gold-colored caps
- **1** 30" (76cm) nylon string
- **2** clamshell bead tips
- **2** crimps
- **2** jump rings
- **1** clasp

The crystals, bead caps, and seed beads used here all have a gold to brownish hue to them. They do not need to be the exact same color to make an attractive necklace.

Earrings

- **2** 0.39" (10mm) oblong pearls
- **4** gold-colored bead caps
- **2** 0.59" (1.5cm) chains
- **4** 0.08" (2mm) gold-colored beads
- **2** gold-colored head pins
- **1** set of earring wires

Bold

What to Do

This necklace is simple and the pearls together with the gold-colored crystals have a very classy look. The strand is just the right thickness; it can enhance any outfit in your wardrobe.

1. Form a simple pattern using these pearls, crystals, and bead caps.

2. When the strand is long enough, add the clamshell bead caps, jump rings, and clasp to finish it off.

Earrings

The pearls covered with gold-colored bead caps have a special shine. Use chains to dangle the pearls at a length that will best accentuate your features. Thread a pearl with two gold-colored bead caps and two gold-colored beads on a head pin. Cut the pin to the desired length. Make a simple loop with the round-nose pliers and attach the loop to one end of the chain (see Section Two: Basic Skills — "Making a Simple Loop"). Connect the other end of the chain to the earring wire. Repeat to make a pair.

Select a chain that is strong enough to hold the 10mm pearls.

It Rocks

Materials

Necklace

- **15** 0.39" (10mm) oblong pearls
- **14** 0.63" (16mm) red Czech glass triangles
- **30** silver-colored seed beads size 11/0
- **1** 30" (76cm) string of nylon
- **2** clamshell bead caps
- **2** crimps
- **2** jump rings
- **1** hook and eye clasp

Extension (optional)
- **1** 0.51 x 0.28" (13 x 7mm) drop pearl
- **2** 0.24" (6mm) SWAROVSKI® ELEMENTS Bead Art .6200 Siam
- **4** 0.39" (10mm) oblong pearls
- **5** eye pins

Earrings
- **2** 0.39" (10mm) oblong pearls
- **2** 0.63" (16mm) red Czech glass triangles
- **44** silver-colored seed beads 11/0

These bright red Czech glass triangles are very attractive. Mix them with these lovely pearls to make a statement.

- **4** 0.24" (6mm) SWAROVSKI® ELEMENTS Bead Art .6200 Siam
- **2** strands of 8" (21cm) silver-colored wire in 26 gauge thickness
- **1** set of earring wires

It Rocks

What to Do

It Rocks is a single strand necklace with a hook and eye clasp plus an extension chain. Follow the pattern in the photo and continue until the desired length is reached.

If you do not want to add the extension chain, then just finish it off with the clasp. If you like the added details of the extension chain, then use the eye pins and pearls to create the chain. Using the eye pin, add one seed bead, one pearl, and then another seed bead before making a simple loop with the round-nose pliers. Make four of these and connect them together to form the extension chain.

End with the drop pearl unit. Using an eye pin, put in a seed bead, two Rivoli beads, and another seed bead. Proceed to bend the pin for the drop pearl. *(see Section Two: Basic Skills — "Wrap Top Drilled Bead")*

This simple pattern combines such lovely colors. What a combination!

Earrings

Using wire, thread through the red triangle. Follow the sketch and step-by-step photos. Use round nose pliers to make a loop. (See "Making a Loop" in *Section Two: Basic Skills*). Connect the earring wire. Make a pair.

Start with the red Czech glass triangle in the middle and proceed with the seed beads on both sides. Thread both wires through the pearl.

Feed seed beads to both sides until you can bring the wire together around the pearl.

Thread both wires through a seed bead, two Rivoli beads, and another seed bead. End by making a wire loop using the round-nose pliers.

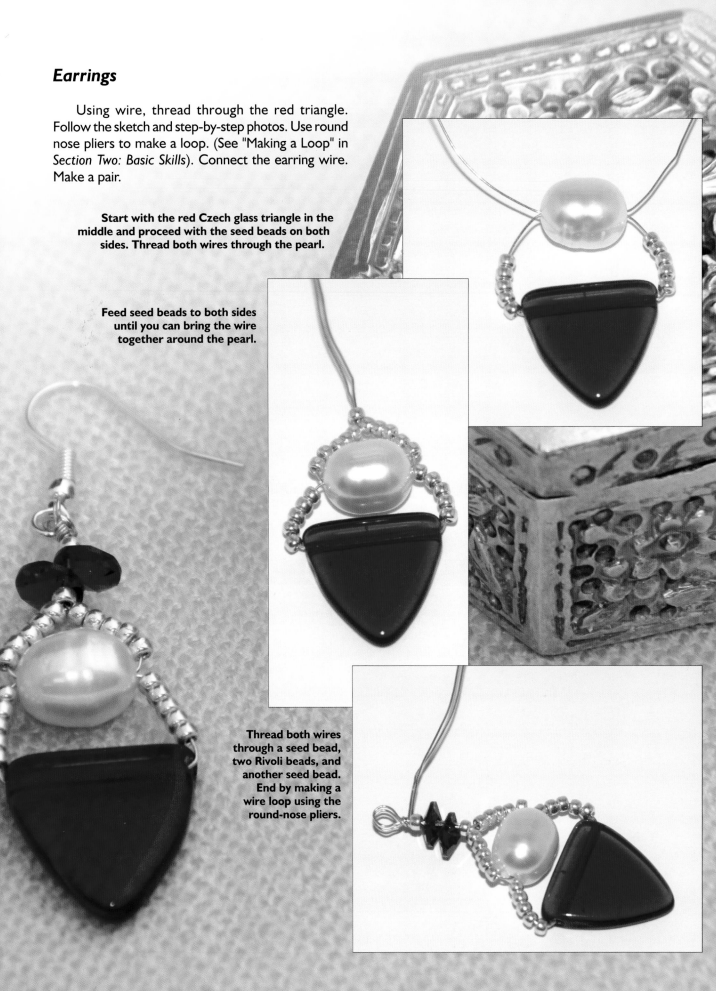

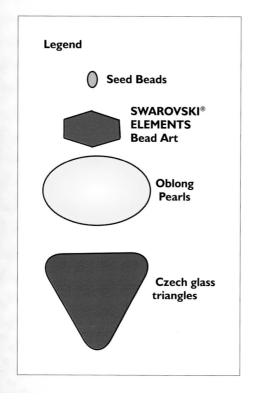

Legend

Seed Beads

**SWAROVSKI®
ELEMENTS**
Bead Art

Oblong
Pearls

Czech glass
triangles

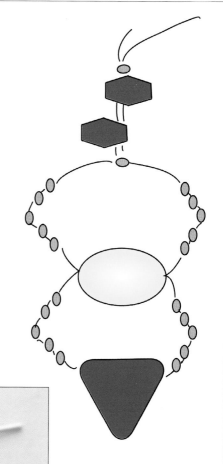

**Check to make sure that the
wires are twisted tight and
the ends are smooth.**

Little Kisses

Materials

Necklace

- **10** 0.39" x 0.43" (10 x 11mm) SWAROVSKI® ELEMENTS Pendant Art .6012 Crystal AB Flat Briolette Pendants
- **10** silver-colored cross tube findings 0.31" (8mm) in length
- **70** pieces 0.20" (5mm) white pearls
- **1** nylon string 45" (115cm)
- **2** clamshell bead tips
- **2** crimps
- **2** jump rings
- **1** clasp

Earrings

- **2** 0.39" x 0.43" (10 x 11mm) SWAROVSKI® ELEMENTS Pendant Art .6012 Crystal AB Flat Briolette Pendants
- **2** silver-colored cross tube findings 0.31" (8mm)
- **12** mini white pearls
- **2** strands of 4" (10cm) silver-colored wire in 26-gauge thickness

Use these Briolette crystals, pearls, and silver-colored findings to make a lovely necklace.

- **2** jump rings
- **1** set of earring wires

Little Kisses

What to Do

Follow the sketch by placing two pearls in between two flat briolette and cross tubes. String a total of ten briolette units, and then add pearls to both sides until the desired length. Finish off by adding the clasp.

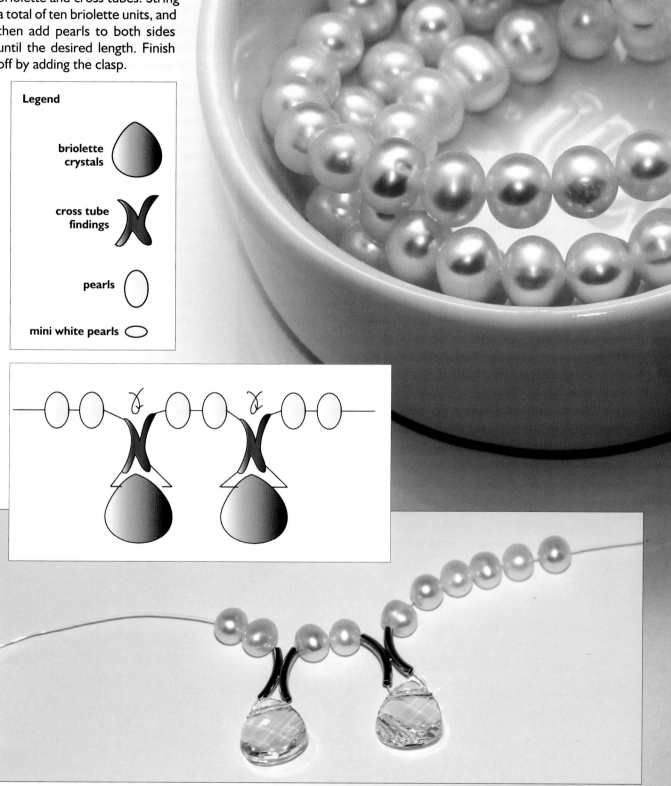

Legend

briolette crystals

cross tube findings

pearls

mini white pearls

Put ten Briolette crystals in front to complete the design.

Earrings

Follow the sketch for the earrings using the fine silver-colored wire.

Use mini pearls of matching color to make these cute, dainty earrings.

Summer Breeze

Materials

Necklace

- **72** 0.24" (6mm) pearls
- **64** 0.31" (8mm) pearls (large pearls)
- **30**+/- mini pearls for balancing length of 3 strands
- **8** 0.24" (6mm) silver-colored rondelles with crystals
- **19** 0.16" (4mm) SWAROVSKI® ELEMENTS Bead Art .530 Pacific Opal
- **11** 0.47" (12mm) large turquoise color Howlite coins
- **34** 0.39" (10mm) small turquoise color Howlite coins
- **3** 30" (76cm) nylon strands
- **6** clamshell bead tips
- **6** crimps
- **2** jump rings
- **1** clasp

Three different types of pearls are used here: similar shapes, but different sizes. If you prefer, you can use just one type of pearl.

Extension (optional)

- **1** 4" (10cm) silver-colored chain
- **1** 0.39" (10mm) small turquoise color Howlite coin
- **1** bead cap
- **1** mini pearl
- **1** 0.16" (4mm) SWAROVSKI® ELEMENTS Bead Art .5301 Pacific Opal
- **1** head pin

Earrings

- **2** 0.47" (12mm) large turquoise color Howlite coins
- **2** bead caps
- **2** 0.31" (8mm) pearls
- **2** 0.16" (4mm) SWAROVSKI® ELEMENTS Bead Art .530 Pacific Opal
- **2** head pins
- **1** set of earring wires

Summer Breeze

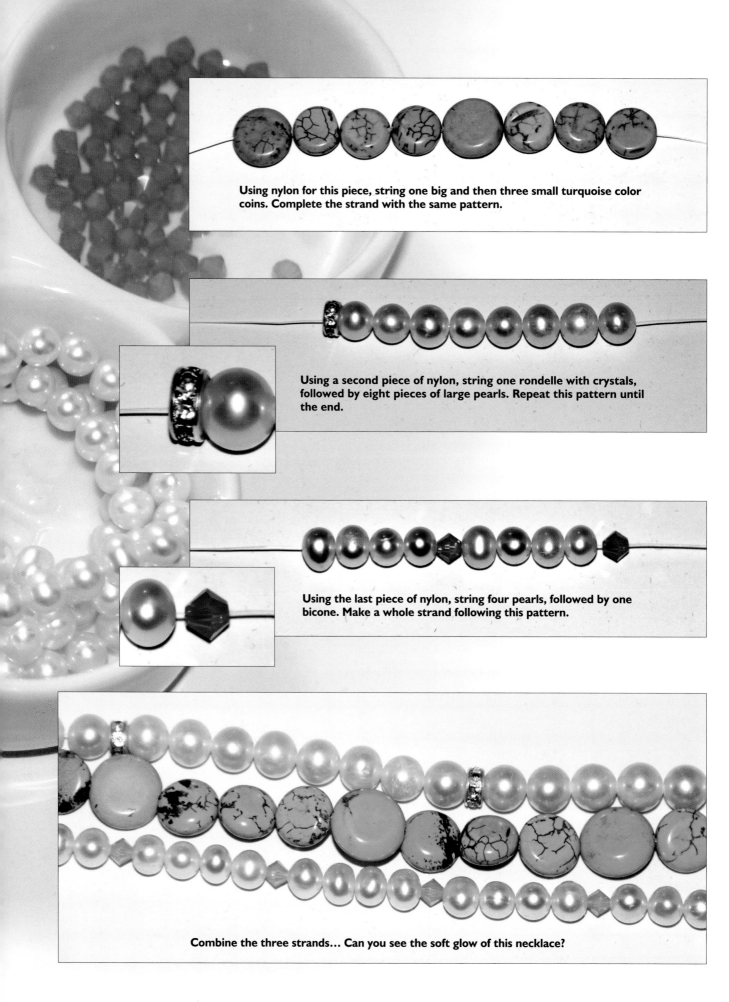

Using nylon for this piece, string one big and then three small turquoise color coins. Complete the strand with the same pattern.

Using a second piece of nylon, string one rondelle with crystals, followed by eight pieces of large pearls. Repeat this pattern until the end.

Using the last piece of nylon, string four pearls, followed by one bicone. Make a whole strand following this pattern.

Combine the three strands... Can you see the soft glow of this necklace?

What to Do

For the sample here, the drop at the end of the extension chain is made with a small coin and mini pearl (see bottom image). The earrings are made with large coins and pearls. Depending on your materials and your preference, you can make something different.

Line the three strands together. Add mini pearls to make them all the same length. End the necklace with clamshell bead caps and finish off the six ends. Then combine the three strands in one jump ring, and on one end add the extension chain and on the other end add the hook.

Note: If you want to twist the three strands to make a thicker rope, you need to provide extra length for the twist and thickness.

Use a head pin. Put the turquoise color coin, bead cap, pearl, and crystal on the pin. Finish with a simple loop on top and connect to the earring wire.

Crown of Copper

One kind of pearl with three different copper findings. There are two types of copper round beads here: the 0.2" (5mm) smooth rounds and the 0.12" (3mm) corrugated rounds.

Materials

Necklace
- **10** 0.39" (10mm) copper floral loops
- **264** 0.16" (4mm) rice pearls (about 2 1/2 strand of 16" rice pearls)
- **3** 30" (76cm) strands of nylon
- **6** clamshell bead tips
- **6** crimps
- **2** jump rings
- **1** clasp

Bracelet
- **9** 0.20" (5mm) copper beads
- **16** 0.12" (3mm) small copper beads
- **97** 0.16" (4mm) rice pearls (about 1 strand of 16" rice pearls)
- **3** 14" (36cm) strands of nylon
- **6** clamshell bead tips
- **6** crimps
- **2** jump rings
- **1** lobster clasp
- **1** extension chain

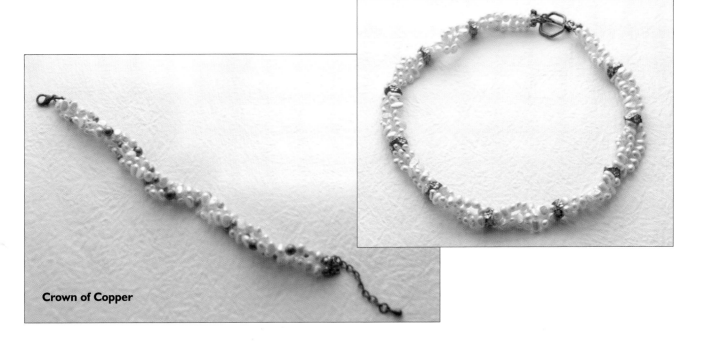

Crown of Copper

What to Do

Both the necklace and bracelet use three strands of rice pearls, but the twist is in the different usage of the copper findings. It makes the set more interesting. The necklace has the copper loops to hold the three strands together, whereas the bracelet is dotted with copper beads at seemingly random but regular intervals.

Necklace

Using three strands of nylons, thread eight rice pearls on each strand and then thread all three through the same copper loop. Repeat pattern until the desired length. End each strand with the clamshell bead tips and crimps. Collect the three strands on one jump ring then connect the jump ring to the clasp. Finish the other end the same way.

Bracelet

Make first strand of bracelet with three pearls and one 0.2" (5mm) copper round beads.
Follow the pattern until you've reached a desirable length for the bracelet.

Make second strand of bracelet with two pearls, one 0.12" (3mm) copper round, four pearls, and another 0.12" (3mm) copper round. Follow the pattern until you've reached a desirable length for the bracelet.

Make last strand of bracelet with five pearls and one 0.12" (3mm) copper round.
Follow the pattern until you've reached a desirable length for the bracelet.

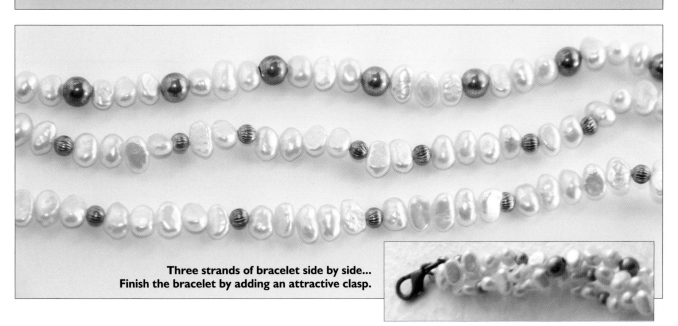

Three strands of bracelet side by side...
Finish the bracelet by adding an attractive clasp.

The Touch

Materials

Necklace

- **46** 0.39 x 0.47" (10 x 12mm) pearls (1 16" strand)
- **4** 0.39" (10mm) SWAROVSKI® ELEMENTS Bead Art .5000 Amethyst
- **4** 0.39" (10mm) SWAROVSKI® ELEMENTS Bead Art .5000 Black Diamond AB
- **16** 925 silver bead caps
- **12** checker motif silver-colored findings
- **8** 1.38" (3.5cm) eye pins
- **2** strands 7" (18cm) Beading wire
- **2** strands 9" (23cm) Beading wire
- **1** 12" (30cm) Beading wire
- **20** crimps
- **1** clasp

Large pearls, 925 silver bead caps, silver-colored findings, and 10mm round crystals in black diamond (**AB**) and amethyst.

The Touch

What to Do

Using an eye pin, start with a bead cap and a 0.39" (10mm) amethyst round crystal. Put on the closing bead cap and make a simple loop *(see Section Two: Basic Skills — "Making a Simple Loop")*. Connect the loop to a checker motif silver-colored finding. Make the same thing using the black diamond round crystals this time. There are four links in total. Each link has one checker finding, one amethyst round crystal unit, another checker finding, one black diamond round crystal unit, and lastly a checker motif finding.

Assemble the pearl strands by stringing pearls on beading wire and secure each end with two crimp beads. There are five strands of these pearls: a pair of twelve pearls near the clasp, a pair of eight pearls on the left and right front, then the longest strand of eighteen pearls in front. Please check the size of the pearls and your preference then adjust accordingly. The finished necklace length in this sample is 35.5" (90cm).

Connect the crystals enclosed in bead caps on eye pins with the silver-colored findings and strands of pearl.

Two-Way Pearl

Materials

Necklace

- **5** strands of pearls in complementing colors of different sizes and shapes
- **3** 30" (75cm) strings of nylon
- **6** clamshell bead tips
- **6** crimps
- **6** jump rings
- **1** 3-row clasp

This sample is done with two strands of gray, two strands of peach, and one strand of white.

Two-Way Pearl

What to Do

Clip three strands of nylon together with a stationary clip and start stringing pearls onto the strands at random. Do a segment of two inches on the first strand and then the next and rotate in this way. Try to monitor the effect of your creation along the way. The basic rule is start in the middle and work towards the sides. Place larger pearls in the middle and leave the smaller ones near the clasp for more comfortable wear. Try to alternate the color of the pearls so that the colors are evenly distributed. When you have reached the desired length and effect, end each strand with clamshell bead caps and secure the ends with crimps. Connect the three strands to the 3-row clasp.

Start with one strand in random colors and shapes.

Line the three strands together to see if the color is spread evenly.

Twist the strands together to see the effect.

Continue to check the look and feel of the necklace as you move along.

Two-Way Pearl (loose)

**Two-Way Pearl
(twisted)**

34

Pearl Chain

Materials

Bracelet

- **10** 0.20 x 0.28" (5 x 7mm) rice pearls
- **1** 24" (60cm) gold-colored fine chain
- **10** eye pins
- **4** small jump rings
- **1** double row gold clasp

Line up the four chains as shown before assembling.

Pearl Chain

What to Do

Cut ten segments of gold chain, each measuring 0.6" (15mm). The easiest way to measure and cut the chain is: Hang them on a pin. Place them at eye level. Cut the chain by measuring against the first chain.

Put one pearl on an eye pin and make a simple loop *(see Section Two: Basic Skills — "Making a Simple Loop")*, and then connect it to a chain segment. Repeat until you have five sections of pearls and five sections of chain on one strand. Make another strand in the same manner. Cut two long gold chain segments to match these two strands of pearl chain. Line them up as shown and adjust if needed. Proceed to put two strands on one jump ring and connect the jump rings to the 2-row clasp. Connect all ends of the four strands and you have a fancy pearl gold chain bracelet.

Distinct

Materials

Necklace

- **1** 2.17" (55mm) Turquoise color Howlite donut
- **10+/-** 0.2" (5mm) SWAROVSKI® ELEMENTS Pearls Art .5810 Light Gray
- **1** 14" (36cm) 26 gauge silver-colored wire
- **1** 17.5" (44.5cm) faux suede
- **2** 925 silver tubes with large holes
- **1** closed ring
- **1** pair of crimp end (coil fastener) with lobster claw and extension

This turquoise color Howlite pendant is a good size charm. Combine the charm with these light gray pearls to make an interesting piece.

Distinct

What to Do

Take the Turquoise donut in hand. Check both sides carefully and decide which side you want to use as front. Thread the silver-colored wire through the hole. Add gray pearls in front, and continue to loop the wire through the hole. Depending on the size of your donut and the size of the pearls, this can create a soothing combination.

When you have achieved the desired effect, proceed to make a loop on top. Loop through a closed ring and twist to tighten the silver-colored wire. Check the tension and trim off the ends. Thread a piece of faux suede through the closed ring. Adjust the length of the faux suede. Add the two silver tubes, one on each side of the charm. Crimp the crimp ends and lobster claw onto the faux suede. Place the lobster claw on right if you are a right-hander and vice-versa if you are a left-hander.

LP

Materials

Necklace
- **18** 0.43 x 0.39" (11 x 10mm) oval pearls
- **51** 0.12" (2-3mm) lapis lazuli round beads
- **85** silver-colored seed beads in 11/0 size
- **2** 0.2" (5mm) spacers
- **2** 28" (70cm) nylon strings
- **2** Clamshell bead tips
- **2** crimps
- **2** jump rings
- **1** hook and ring clasp

Extension (optional)
- **1** 0.43 x 0.39" (11 x 10mm) oval pearl
- **1** 0.12" (2-3mm) lapis lazuli round
- **1** silver-colored seed bead 11/0
- **1** head pin
- **1** 4" (10cm) chain

The Oval pearls, silver-colored seed beads, and Lapis Lazuli round beads give a very classy look. It looks great with any suit or dress.

Bracelet
- **6** 0.43" x 0.39" (11 x 10mm) oval pearls
- **15** 0.12" (2-3mm) lapis lazuli
- **29** silver-colored seed beads 11/0
- **2** 0.2" (5mm) spacers
- **2** 14" (36cm) nylon
- **2** clamshell bead tips
- **2** crimps and **2** jump rings
- **1** toggle clasp

Earrings
- **2** 0.43 x 0.39" (11 x 10mm) oval pearls
- **6** 0.12" (2-3mm) lapis lazuli
- **8** silver-colored seed beads 11/0
- **2** 5" (13cm) 26 gauge silver-colored wires
- **1** pair of earring wires

LP

Legend

○ seed beads

● lapis lazuli

◯ oval pearls

What to Do

Necklace and Bracelet

Both the LP necklace and bracelet are done with two strands of nylon. Begin by threading two strands of nylon through an oval pearl. Refer to the sketch and weave the pearls, seed beads, and lapis lazuli beads on until the desired length is reached. Add spacers to adjust the length if necessary. End with a clamshell bead tip and follow the standard single strand procedures *(see Section Two: Basic Skills — "Ending a Single Strand")*. Just thread both strands of nylon through the clamshell bead tip, crimp, and hide the ends.

Use two pieces of nylon and string the beads together.

Earrings

Use the wire to string the pearls, seed beads, and lapis lazuli beads together as depicted in the sketch, and then connect to the earring wire. Check to make sure the ends are secure. Repeat to make a pair.

Pick up the wire and thread through the pearl, seed beads, and Lapis Lazuli beads. Twist the top and make a loop with the round-nose pliers.

Check that the wires are tight and make sure the ends are well hidden.

Picture Perfect

Materials

Necklace

- **8** 0.79" (20mm) silver-colored findings (large spacers)
- **9** 0.31" (8mm) SWAROVSKI® ELEMENTS Bead Art .5000 Jet
- **18** silver-colored spacers
- **72** 0.20" (5mm) small pearls (1 strand 16")
- **92** 0.24" (6mm) pearls (1 + strand 16")
- **2** 0.35" (9mm) silver-colored spacer
- **2** 41" (104cm) nylon strings
- **2** clamshell bead tips
- **2** crimps
- **2** jump rings
- **1** silver-colored clasp

When you weave pearls together, the strand looks a lot thicker. This is a good way to create an expensive-looking piece of jewelry with smaller pearls.

Earrings

- **2** 0.79" (20mm) silver-colored findings (large spacers)
- **2** 0.31" (8mm) SWAROVSKI® ELEMENTS Bead Art .5000 Jet
- **4** spacers
- **2** 0.24" (6mm) pearls
- **2** head pins
- **2** eye pins
- **1** set of earring wires

Picture Perfect

Legend

- ● **spacers**
- ○ **small pearls**
- ○ **pearls**
- ◉ **crystals**
- ⬭ **large spacers**

What to Do

Necklace

Take two pieces of nylon and follow the pattern in the sketch. Repeat the pattern until you reach the desired length. End with the round spacers then clamshell bead tips. Attach the clasp.

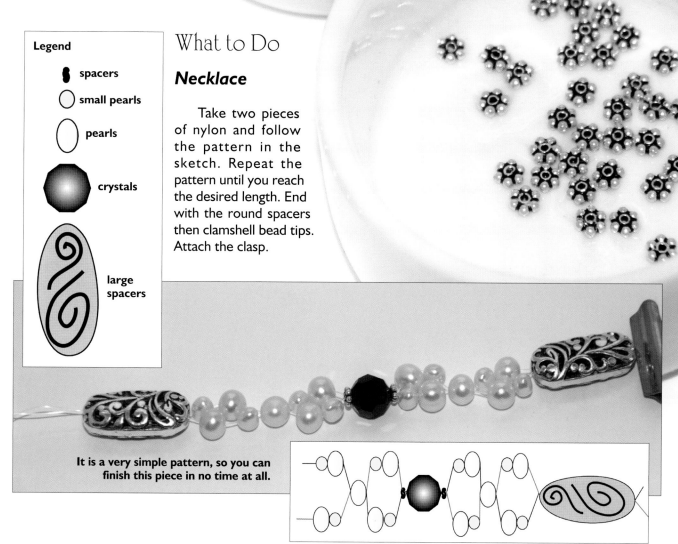

It is a very simple pattern, so you can finish this piece in no time at all.

Check regularly to make sure that the pattern is correct.

Earrings

Use a head pin. Pick up a pearl, and a crystal enclosed in bead caps. Trim and make a simple loop with the round-nose pliers. Close the loop on an eye pin. Thread a silver finding, trim and make a simple loop and hook onto the earring wire. Repeat to make a pair (see Section Two: Basic Skills — "Making a Simple Loop").

Do the earrings with head pins and eye pins.

Athens

The pearls here are top drilled. They create a very different look.

Materials

Necklace

- **4** strands 0.20 x 0.28" (5 x 7mm) oblong top drilled pearls
- **12** 0.31" (8mm) SWAROVSKI® ELEMENTS Bead Art .5000 Light Colorado AB
- **30** 0.16" (4mm) SWAROVSKI® ELEMENTS Bead Art .5301 Topaz
- **2** large gold-colored bead caps
- **3** 24" (60cm) strands of nylon
- **2** gold-colored clamshell bead tips
- **2** crimps
- **2** gold-colored jump rings
- **1** 1.5" (38mm) gold-colored clasp

Earrings

- **12** 0.20 x 0.28" (5 x 7mm) oblong top drilled pearls
- **16** 0.16" (4mm) SWAROVSKI® ELEMENTS Bead Art .5301 Topaz
- **4** gold-colored head pins
- **2** 6" (15cm) 26 gauge gold-colored wires
- **1** set of earring wires

Athens

What to Do

Necklace

Legend

⬭ pearls

◆ bicones

⬣ crystals

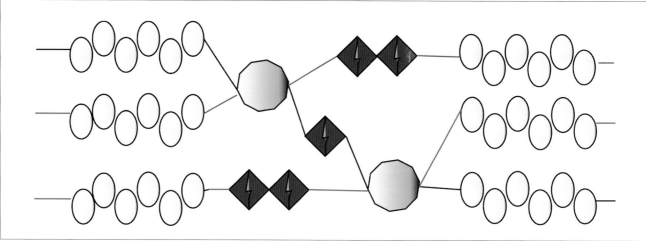

Take three pieces of nylon and string the pearls. Following the sketch pattern, thread ten pearls on each strand. Check the pattern along the way.

Twist the strands together to see the effect.

When you reach the desired length, cap all three strands with a bead cap. Follow with a clamshell bead tip, and proceed to tie the knots and hide each tail among the pearls. Add on a beautiful clasp to finish the piece.

Earrings

Follow the sketch and step-by-step photos.
Use round nose pliers to make a simple loop (similar to "Making a Simple Loop" in *Section Two: Basic Skills*) to complete the earrings.

Use the wire to make a loop with the round-nose pliers. Do a couple of twist. Put in four bicone beads on each side.

End with a simple loop on top.

Add two head pins filled with pearls to complete each earring.

Simple Triangle

Materials

Necklace
- **21** 0.39" (10mm) antique copper-colored oblong spacers
- **117** 0.20" (5mm) rice pearls (1 + strand)
- **1** 54" (140cm) nylon
- **2** copper-colored clamshell bead tips
- **2** crimps
- **2** copper-colored jump rings
- **1** lobster clasp
- **1** extension chain
- **1** head pin

Extension (optional)
- **2** pearls
- **1** copper spacer

This very simple piece only uses two types of beads: Pearls and oblong antique copper-colored beads.

Earrings
- **4** 0.39" (10mm) antique copper-colored oblong spacers
- **14** 0.20" (5mm) rice pearls
- **2** 8" (20cm) nylon strings
- **2** copper-colored clamshell bead tips
- **2** crimps
- **1** set of copper-colored earring wires

Simple Triangle

What to Do

Simple Triangle is basically done with one long strand of nylon that loops back to form the triangle pearl patterns. If you want the necklace to end with a v-drop in front, then use another piece of nylon and add one pearl to finish it off. *(You will need an odd number of triangle pearl patterns on the completed necklace strand to make it a balanced necklace.)* With the same logic, you can make the whole strand much longer and add the pearl in between the antique copper-colored spacers to make a fancier piece.

Necklace

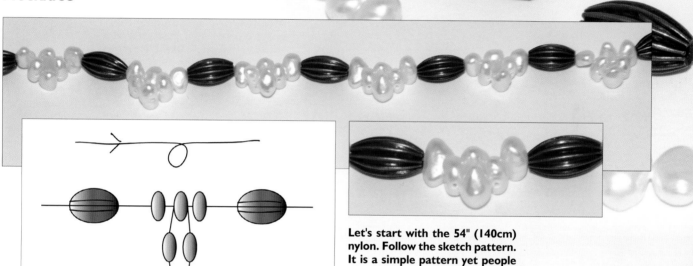

Basic Pattern

Let's start with the 54" (140cm) nylon. Follow the sketch pattern. It is a simple pattern yet people will think that you have toiled for hours to come up with this necklace.

Legend

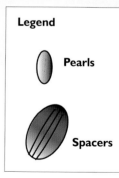

Pearls

Spacers

The 'V' Drop

Adding the v-shape drop is very easy. Using another piece of nylon, thread through the beads as shown on the sketch. Add the extra pearl in the middle. Thread through the beads on the other side. Check the balance and effect and then tie the knots to secure the v-shape drop. Tie the double knot go through a few beads and then tie a single knot. Finish off by hiding the tail in the beads.

V-Drop

Earrings

Follow the simple pattern on the sketch. Finish with the clamshell bead tip and a crimp bead inside, and then connect to the earring wire. Repeat to make a pair. The beads are very light, so the nylon with a crimp can hold the structure. Be sure to crimp the bead real tight.

Moon Rock

Materials

Ring

- **1** 0.55" (14mm) coin pearl
- **1** 0.20" (5mm) pearl
- **10**+/- 0.08" (2mm) 925 silver beads
- **1** 5" (13 cm) silver wire about 18 gauge
- **1** 7" (18 cm) silver-colored wire 26 gauge

For this project, you'll need a coin pearl, 0.20" (5mm) round pearl, and 0.08" (2mm) round silver beads. The mandrel is essential in making a good ring.

Moon Rock

What to Do

Find a ring that is your desirable size, slide it onto the wooden mandrel, and mark its place.

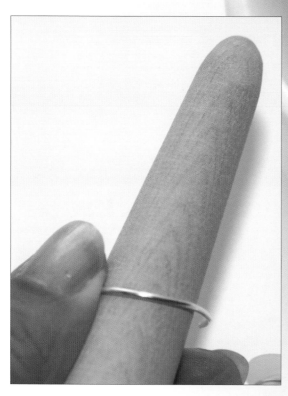

Wrap the 18-gauge silver wire round the mandrel using the marking as reference point. The wire is soft; you can use your bare hands to make the ring loop.

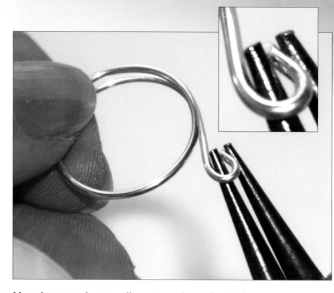

File the end of the wire with a file to smooth the end.

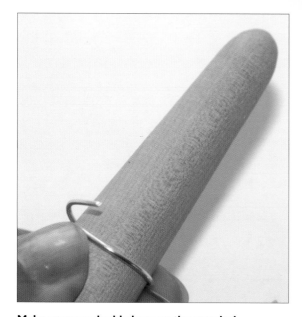

Make an open double loop on the mandrel.

Use the round-nose pliers to make a simple loop.

Measure the coin pearl on the ring space and cut the wire.

Make another simple loop on the other end of the wire.
Adjust the loops to line up nicely.

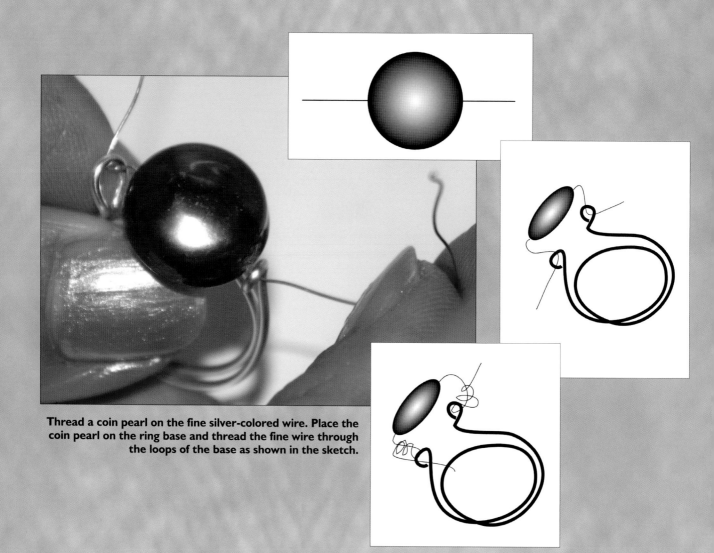

Thread a coin pearl on the fine silver-colored wire. Place the coin pearl on the ring base and thread the fine wire through the loops of the base as shown in the sketch.

Add the pearl and silver beads on the fine wire. Adjust the number to cover the top of your coin pearl. Anchor to the loop of the other side. Use a pair of chain-nose pliers to pull it tight.

Add three more silver beads to finish the design, and then twist the fine wire to secure and hide the ends.

Legend

○ silver beads

● pearls

● coin pearls

Royal Gold

The pearls used here are oblong and top drilled. The pearls on the earrings are different; they are perpendicularly drilled.

Materials

Necklace

- **24** 0.35 x 0.39" (9 x 10mm) top drilled pearls
- **7** 0.31" (8mm) gold-colored spacers
- **10** 0.24" (6mm) fire polish gold beads
- **10** 0.12" (3mm) gold-colored beads
- **5** gold-colored coil findings
- **31** eye pins
- **5** 5" (13cm) gold-colored wires 26 gauge
- **2** jump rings
- **1** clasp

Earrings

- **2** 0.31" (8mm) pearls perpendicular drilled
- **2** 0.31" (8mm) gold-colored spacers
- **2** gold-colored coil findings
- **2** head pins
- **1** pair of gold-colored earring wires

Royal Gold

What to Do

Necklace

Make the royal gold unit with the gold-colored fine wire. Follow the photo and string the beads onto the wire.

Form a circle with the wire by going through the top three beads again.

Tighten the wire with a pair of chain-nose pliers. Use the round-nose pliers to make a simple loop at one end.

Tighten the other end. Trim off the excess wire. Finish with another simple loop.

To Finish:

Using an eye pin, put on one pearl and then make a simple loop with the round-nose pliers *(see Section Two: Basic Skills — "Making a Simple Loop")*. Connect three pearl units with one Royal Gold unit. Repeat until you have five Royal Gold units in the chain, ending with three pearl units on both ends. Put a gold-colored spacer on an eye pin and make a simple loop; make two of these. Attach these to the two ends of the chain. Check the length. Add more pearl units if needed. Connect the ends to jump rings and then attach the clasp.

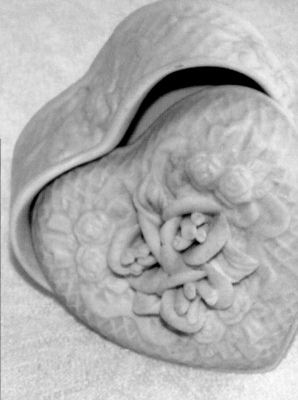

Using the head pin, put on a pearl, gold coil, and spacer. Use the round-nose pliers to make a simple loop and hook onto the earring wire.

Trillium

Materials

Necklace
- **7** 0.51" (13mm) antique bronze-colored flowers (3 rings in the back)
- **7** 0.67" (17mm) antique S-shaped bronze-colored connectors
- **4** 0.24" (6mm) diamond-shaped antique bronze-colored spacers
- **1** 0.31 x 0.43" (8 x 11mm) drop pearl
- **29** 0.20" (5mm) potato pearls
- **16** eye pins
- **2** jump rings
- **1** clasp

Earrings
- **4** 0.51" (13mm) antique bronze-colored flowers (3 rings in the back)
- **12** 0.20" (5mm) potato pearls
- **4** 6" (15cm) nylon strings
- **2** S-shaped connectors
- **2** jump rings

You will be using three types of bronze-colored findings and pearls, plus bronze-colored eye and head pins, to make this chain necklace set.

- **1** pair of earring wires

Ring
- **1** 0.51" (13mm) flower finding
- **6** 0.20" (5mm) potato pearls
- **1** 5" (13cm) 18-gauge antique bronze-colored wire approximate (depending on ring size)
- **1** 8" (20cm) 26 gauge wire

Trillium

What to Do

Trillium is an interesting piece. When you have some pearls left from other projects, you can still come up with a lovely set by adding interesting findings. You can come up with many different combinations. Lay out the pieces on a beading board to check the length and design before you assemble everything.

Necklace

Compose this center piece with a drop pearl. If you do not have a drop pearl, you can substitute it with a round pearl on a head pin.

Make two pairs of this piece (total four pieces). Note that the flower has three rings on the back. Leave the unconnected ring pointing outwards.

Make one pair of this piece.

Make these two pieces to form a pair.

Connect these three together to form a "Y" for the front of the necklace.

Join these pieces together first and then connect to the "Y." Do the same for the other side of the "Y." Now the necklace is complete. Check the length; please adjust by adding or removing a unit. When you are happy with the design, connect the clasp to the ends.

Earrings

Pick up a flower. Follow the sketch; use nylon to string the pearls on its back. Add another flower to cover and thread the nylon string through the second flower and the same set of pearls. Tighten and secure the nylon.

Connect the piece to an S-shaped connector and the earring wire to finish. Repeat to make a pair.

Compare the pair... make sure they are balanced and front facing.

Ring

Legend

pearls

flower finding

Use the fine gold-colored wire to thread the pearls and the flower together as shown in the sketch. Prepare the ring base as in the "Moon Rock" project. Use a bronze-colored wire to match the flower. Connect the points and hide the ends in the back of the ring.

Garnet Blossoms

Materials

Watch

- **1** watch face
- **5** 0.43 x 0.75" (11 x 19mm) oval shape pearls
- **42** 0.24" (6mm) garnet chips
- **12** seed beads 11/0
- **2** 18" (46cm) nylon strings
- **2** jump rings
- **2** closed rings
- **1** clasp

Simple but attractive combination: Garnet chips, with silver seed beads, and oval pearls.

Garnet Blossoms

What to Do

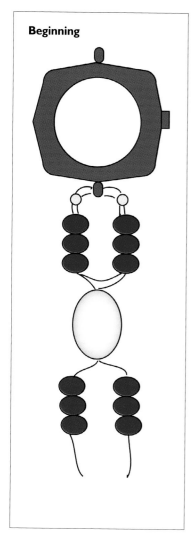

Beginning

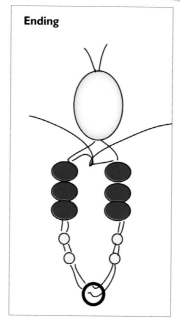

Ending

Legend

- ○ seed beads
- ● garnet chips
- ⬭ oval pearls
- ◯ closed ring

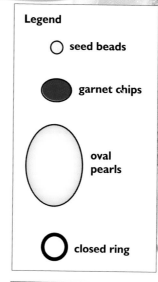

Follow the drawings. Use one strand of nylon at each side of the watch strap. Both sides follow the same pattern. Attach the toggle and bar when you have reached the desired length.

Finesse

Materials

Watch

- **1** watch face
- **4** 2-hole spacer bars 0.43" (11mm) in width
- **20** 0.08" (2mm) 925 silver round beads
- **40** 0.20" (5mm) gray pearls
- **4** 12" (30cm) nylon strings
- **2** jump rings
- **2** closed rings
- **1** clasp

**Watches with gray pearls are really hard to find...
You'll attract a lot of compliments wearing this piece.**

Finesse

What to Do

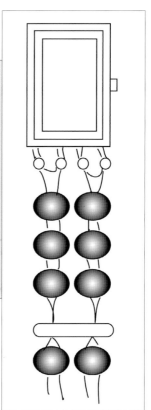

This watch face has three holes on either sides. Using two strands of nylon for each side, thread the beads by following the sketches. The pattern is the same for both sides. Attach the clasp when you have reached the desired length.

Legend

○ silver beads

⬤ gray pearls

▭ 2-holes spacer bars

○ closed rings

End the watch band with silver beads. String the enclosed ring at the end and then connect to the toggle clasp.

Apollo

Materials

Necklace

- **7** 0.71" (18mm) SWAROVSKI® ELEMENTS Bead Art .3221 Crystal Golden Shadow Twist Sew-on Stones
- **8** 0.16" (4mm) SWAROVSKI® ELEMENTS Bead Art .5301 Light Smoked Topaz Bicones
- **8** 0.16" (4mm) SWAROVSKI® ELEMENTS Bead Art .5301 Crystal Effect Dorado 2x Bicones
- **64** 0.28" (7mm) French wires
- **32** 0.16" (4mm) gold-colored findings

Six different components are required to make this necklace, but you will see very soon that this piece is worth the effort.

- **96** 0.16" (4mm) rice pearls
- **16** 8" (20cm) nylon strings
- **2** gold-colored jump rings
- **1** gold-colored clasp

Apollo

What to Do

The necklace is done in segments. Complete the first segments as shown in the picture. Follow the pattern on the sketch, tighten, and hide the ends. Two different colors of 0.16" (4mm) bicone crystals are used here. You can alternate the top and bottom color to make the piece more interesting. Proceed with the next segment by adding one Sew-on twist crystal at a time. When you reach the desired length, use two jump rings instead of the Sew-on twist crystals. Attach the jump rings to the clasp.

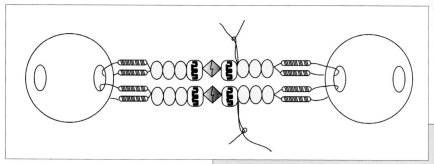

Legend

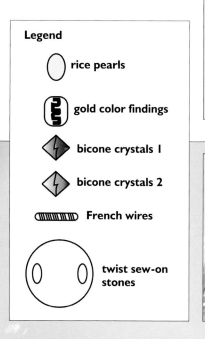

- ◯ rice pearls
- ▤ gold color findings
- ◈ bicone crystals 1
- ◈ bicone crystals 2
- ▭ French wires
- ◯ twist sew-on stones

Make the first unit with two Twist Sew-on Stones as shown in the sketch.

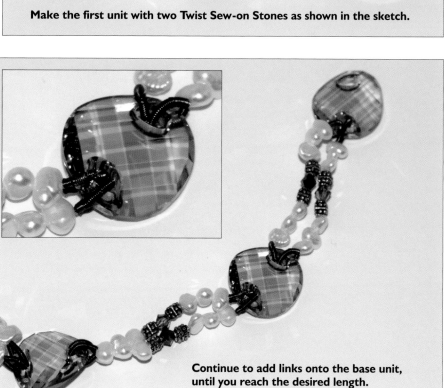

Continue to add links onto the base unit, until you reach the desired length.

Northern Star

Phone charm is a small item. You can make use of leftover pearls or crystals from other projects.

Materials

Phone Charm

- **14** 0.20" (5mm) SWAROVSKI® ELEMENTS Pearls Art .5810 White
- **25** 0.08" (2mm) SWAROVSKI® ELEMENTS Pearls Art .5810 White
- **1** 0.31" (8mm) SWAROVSKI® ELEMENTS Bead Art .5000 Crystal
- **2** Strands of 14" (36cm) nylon
- **1** clamshell bead cap
- **1** crimp
- **1** phone charm finding

Northern Star

What to Do

Start with two nylon threads. Complete Steps 1 and 2, and then add a 0.08" (2mm) round pearl on the tail end. End the piece with a clamshell bead cap and crimp bead. Crimp the bead tight and close the clamshell. Connect to a phone charm finding to finish the piece. Bind off the strings around the star by doing a double knot and pass the strings through a few beads. Do a single knot, then hide the tails and trim off.

Following the sketch, make the main body.

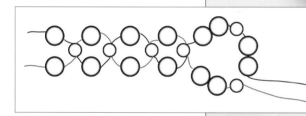

Legend

⭕ small pearls

⭕ pearls

🔶 crystals

Add the small pearls around the main body to make it pretty.

Add a crystal in the middle to complete the design.

74

Sweet Delight

Materials

Necklace

- **3** 0.28 x 0.59" (7 x 15mm) drop pearls
- **4** mini pearls
- **35** 0.20" (5mm) pearls
- **11** 0.24" (6mm) SWAROVSKI® ELEMENTS Bead Art .5003 Crystal AB
- **4** Star findings with AB crystals embedded
- **8** Square flower findings with AB crystals embedded
- **3** 6" (15cm) silver-colored wire in 26 gauge
- **61** eye pins
- **4** jump rings
- **1** 2-row clasp

It is best to get everything ready before starting a project. There are only six components for this fancy necklace. Sweet Delight is a double chain necklace, thus we have to use 2-row findings.

Earrings

- **2** 0.28 x 0.59" (7 x 15mm) drop pearls
- **2** SWAROVSKI® ELEMENTS Bead Art .5003 0.24" (6mm) Crystal AB
- **8** mini pearls
- **4** star findings
- **2** 6" (15cm) silver-colored wire in 26 gauge
- **1** set of earring wires

Sweet Delight

What to Do

Reserve a pair of matching drop-pearls for the earrings, and choose another pair for the left and right drop-pearls for the front of the necklace. Follow the step-by-step photos to make the units, and assemble the necklace and earrings.

Start with this center front unit. Use the fine silver-colored wire to thread the drop pearl, mini pearls, findings, and crystals. Make two side by side loops at the ends.

Make six of these to form the two sides of the three front triangular drop.

Connect these five pieces to form the front triangular drop.

Make seven of these to link to the square
flower findings to form the inner chain.

Make two of these to be placed on
either side of the center drop pearl.

Connect these five pieces to form the left and right triangular
drop. The inner square flower findings are the ones shared with
the front triangular drop.

Make these and connect them together. Then connect another set of four to form the
mirror image of these. Connect these to the back of the left and right triangular drop.
Link the inner chain with the three-pearl chains to complete the necklace. Add the clasp.

Use the fine silver-colored wire to string the beads together. Make two for the set of earrings.

Twist the wires to form one loop, and connect it to the earring wire. Check that the wires are secure and the ends are trimmed properly.

Lacy Flow

Materials

Necklace

- **101** 0.20" (5mm) SWAROVSKI® ELEMENTS Pearls Art .5810 Light Gray
- **100** 0.20" (5mm) SWAROVSKI® ELEMENTS Pearls Art .5810 White
- **5** 0.20" (5mm) SWAROVSKI® ELEMENTS Bead Art .5000 Satin Crystal
- **15** 0.08" (2mm) SWAROVSKI® ELEMENTS Bead Art .5000 Silver Shadow

Take the time to select the colors of your choice. The combination here is very soft and shiny. It goes with any outfit.

- **17** 0.08" (2mm) SWAROVSKI® ELEMENTS Pearls Art .5810 White
- **6** 2-row spacer bar

- **2** 0.31 x 0.43" (8 x 11mm) SWAROVSKI® ELEMENTS Pearl Art .5821 Light Gray
- **2** 52" (132cm) nylon strings

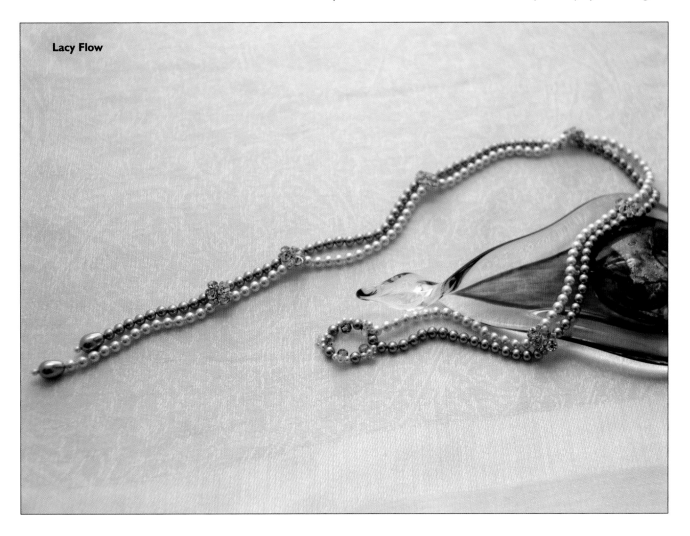

Lacy Flow

What to Do

After finishing Steps 1 and 2, proceed with the double strand. After threading sixteen gray pearls on one strand and sixteen white pearls on the other, slip both strands through a 2-row space bar. Repeat until you have five space bars on the strands.

Do a short segment with six gray pearls and six white pearls. Add another space bar. Add ten more gray pearls on the gray strand, end it with one gray drop pearl and a 0.08" (2mm) white pearl.

To make it more interesting, we will make the white strand longer by adding fourteen white pearls and end it with a gray drop pearl and an 0.08" (2 mm) white pearl.

To finish off, tighten the double strands of drop pearls and hide the endings. Tie the loose ends at the ring end and hide the endings.

Starting with two nylon strings in hand, follow the sketch and finish Steps 1 and 2.

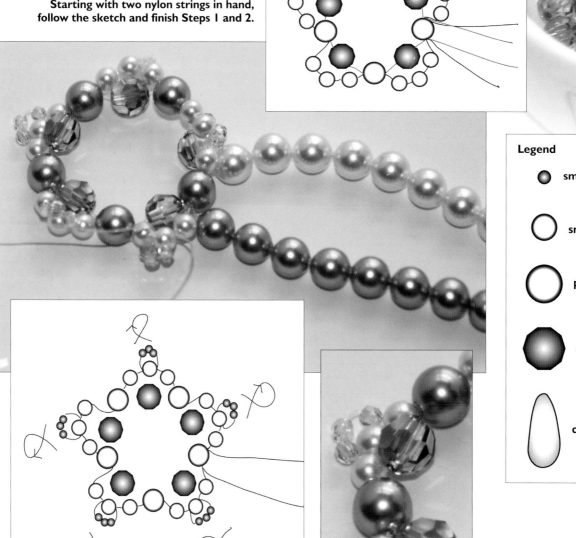

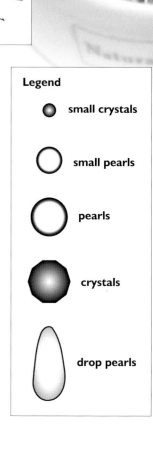

Legend

⬤ small crystals

◯ small pearls

◯ pearls

⬤ crystals

⬭ drop pearls

Continue with the double strand... Check the length and the pattern throughout.

ENDING

The two space bars frame
the ring and ensure that
the necklace stays in place.

2

What
You
Need
to
Know

Your Beads and Tools

Beads

If you visit the same bead store a month after your first visit, you will find many new items. The beader's world is expanding fast. Get inspired at the bead stores.

Seed Beads

Seed beads are small, shiny, and colorful… a great compliment to any piece of work. They can be woven into stunning pieces.

CREATE YOUR STYLE with SWAROVSKI® ELEMENTS

When you walk into any bead shop, you can find attractive SWAROVSKI® ELEMENTS. The shop may not carry all the items available from Swarovski, but you can definitely find some popular items on display. You will be amazed about the variety, colors, shapes, and quality of SWAROVSKI® ELEMENTS. I like to stock up on the colors: jet, clear crystal, golden shadow, and white opal. They can dress up any piece that I am putting together and are neutral enough that they go with everything. You will be surprised at what a difference these crystals can make: they sparkle and shine. You can be working on a gemstones necklace and, when you add some SWAROVSKI® ELEMENTS here and there, you get a totally different feel. The best part is that they last. You just clean them with mild soapy water, and the shine will come right back. They are definitely worth the money.

Czech Glass Beads and Crystal Beads

There is a long history of glass and crystal making in the Czech Republic. There are beautiful colors and shapes and these beads are very durable.

Precious Metal Beads

There are 925 silver, silver coated, and gold plated beads. They can be costly. However, if you are doing something classy and valuable, it is worth the investment. There are findings and clasps available in precious metal as well.

Metal Beads

Metal beads are also called spacers. They add sparkle and interest to your piece. They also help to give a smoother flow when you are using large beads. At the turn, larger beads create a gap and spacer beads help to fill in the gap. When you are a couple of beads short in making a necklace, spacer beads can help to fill in the gaps too.

Semi-precious Stones

Semi-precious beads come in all shapes and sizes. There is a great variation in prices. If you want to start with something economical, the semi-precious stone chips are a good choice.

Glass Beads

There are different kinds of glass beads: the most famous ones are the Murano glass beads from Italy. They have a long history. These specialists maintain the family secret of glass making within a small group. They are very colorful and come in all shapes and sizes.

Indian glass beads are a lot more affordable and can be very appealing, as they are handmade and come with different color accent lines and embellishments.

Ceramic Beads

Ceramic beads have a rustic feel to them. The size of the hole is usually larger, thus very suitable for the faux suede or leather thong kind of necklace.

Plastic beads

Plastic beads are lightweight. They are especially good when you are looking for something more chunky and colorful to create a funky look.

Wood and Shell beads

Wood and shell beads have been around for a long time. Wearing jewelry made of these natural materials makes you feel one with nature.

Pearls

Fresh Water Pearls

These have become a lot more affordable. To determine the quality of pearls, look at the luster, shape, and size. The shinier, the rounder, the bigger they are, the better the quality of pearls. You can start with the budget friendly pearls first then move to the bigger and better ones after you are used to working with pearls. If you have a strand of beautiful pearls, all you have to do is string it together, put on a beautiful clasp, and wear it. If you have some heirloom pearls or semi-precious stone necklaces that you have grown tired of, you can create a new look by stranding a new piece together.

Crystal Pearls

So far, I have only heard of SWAROVSKI® Crystal Pearls'. There is a wide range of colors, shapes and sizes available. There are always new items becoming available, so be on the lookout. They are definitely well made and durable. The holes are comparatively large and uniform. You can thread two or more beading nylons through one SWAROVSKI® Crystal Pearls. They are great for weave designs.

Plastic Pearls

There are many different varieties and quality of plastic pearls. They are never scratch proof; I tend to prefer those that are heavier in weight. They will drape more evenly on your neck. There is no limit to the colors you can find in this category. As I can never be sure of the quality of this type of pearls, I don't use them anymore.

Tools

The good news is that you do not need many tools for beading, but you should look for better quality tools as they last and can make life a lot easier. You don't have to worry though; the tools are not that expensive and you can build up your tool kit and bead supplies bit by bit. The very basic tools that you need would be a pair of wire cutters, a pair of round-nose pliers, a pair of flat-nose pliers, and a pair of pointed-nose pliers.

Maintain the tools well and they will last you a long time. Use the right tools for the right task, and keep them cleaned and oiled. I use AutoSol® to clean my tools — it has done magic for me.

Wire Cutters

Call for the expert when cutting wire — and use a proper pair of cutters. A small one is easier on your hands when you need to cut a lot of head and eye pins for a chain link project.

Round-nose Pliers

This is the tool that you need to make the simple loop on head and eye pins. It is easy to use and you can get used to it in no time.

Pointed-nose and Flat-nose Pliers

Use any two of these pliers to open or close a jump ring. Use any one of these to tighten the crimp beads.

Nylon Jaw Chain-nose Pliers

This nylon jaw will not scratch or damage wire or metal findings. Good for straightening wire. It is very useful when you do wire work designs.

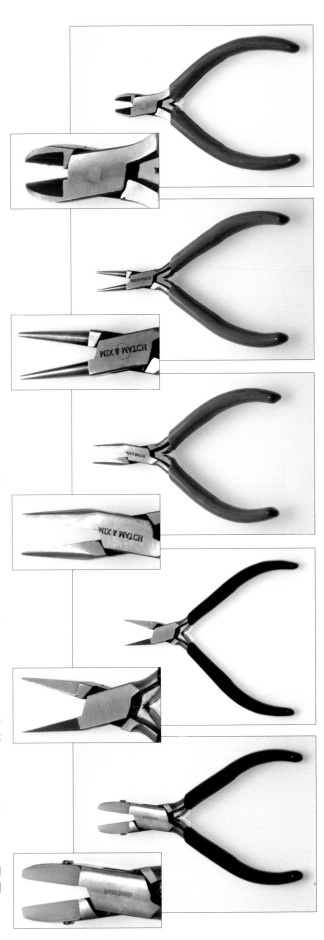

Clips

Beading Board

Miscellaneous Items

There are a few other tools I would recommend, as they can really help move a project along.

- A *beading board* is good to have, as it lets you visualize your project.

- A *beading mat* stops the bead from rolling off.

- *Clips* are wonderful… they are like an extra pair of hands.

- Use *precision tools-bead gauges* to measure beads, jump rings, head or eye pins.

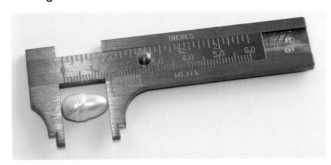

Precision Tool – Bead Gauge

Stringing Materials

You can use anything to string beads together. The popular ones are nylon, elastic, beading wire, tiger tail, leather, and faux suede. The rule of the game is the size of the bead hole and the thickness of the stringing material. If you like the look of leather and suede, you would have to find beads with bigger holes.

Wire

Fine wires are used for wire crochet. They are also useful in making earrings and rings. Thicker wires are harder to bend, but they will hold their shape well. They are ideal for rings. Use the mandrel to help shape the ring.

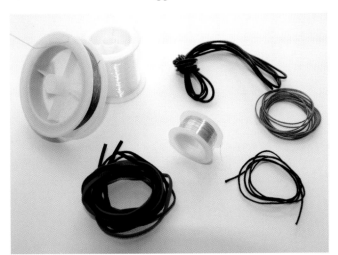

Stringing Materials. Clockwise from top left: beading wire, nylon spool, thick and fine leather cords, faux suede, and fine beading wire.

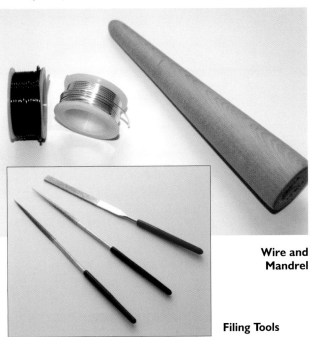

Wire and Mandrel

Filing Tools

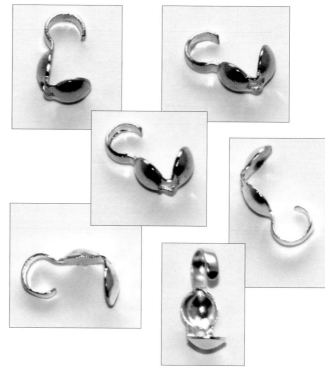

Findings

Most findings can be grouped into four major colors: silver, gold, copper, and black. To complete a project, it's best to have matching color findings. There may be variation of colors within the groups; there are shinier silver (silver plated) and regular silver (rhodium plated and alloy). Rhodium plated findings are great also as the color will stay. You may want to get nickel free findings, if you are allergic to nickel.

Crimps

These tiny metal tubes are extremely useful. You can use them to space focal beads on your wire or chain. You can also use these to fasten the ending of a necklace on beading wire and connect the necklace to the clasp.

Clamshell Bead Tips (Calottes)

These are great tools to use at the ends of a strand: hide the knot and connect to the clasp. Be gentle on the clamshell bead tips and never skim on these for if they break you need to redo the whole piece again.

Clasps

Lobster clasps are economical and suitable for most everyday pieces. If you want to make a statement on your piece, you can spend time to select a toggle, or button clasp to enhance the piece. Magnetic ones are easy to close and most ideal for bracelets.

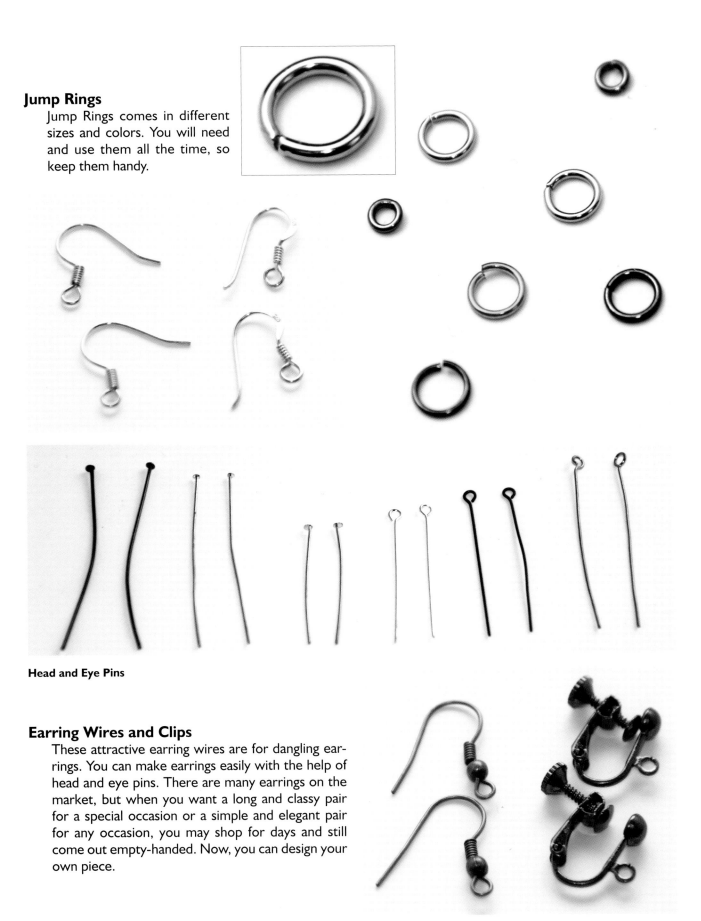

Jump Rings

Jump Rings comes in different sizes and colors. You will need and use them all the time, so keep them handy.

Head and Eye Pins

Earring Wires and Clips

These attractive earring wires are for dangling earrings. You can make earrings easily with the help of head and eye pins. There are many earrings on the market, but when you want a long and classy pair for a special occasion or a simple and elegant pair for any occasion, you may shop for days and still come out empty-handed. Now, you can design your own piece.

Bead Caps

These are great tools to dress up any beads, as the beads look so different in them. The practical use of the bead caps is one to protect the bead from rubbing against the next bead, and two on the occasion when the bead hole is too large; bead caps help to cover up the holes.

Spacer Bars

Spacer bars are great for watchbands and double-stranded necklaces or bracelets.

Leather Crimps

Use the right size for the particular thickness of leather that you are using. Try to match the color to the charm too.

Spacers

These metal beads are useful as fillers. They add sparkle and interest to any piece. The 925 Silver Spacers will last you a long time. They age with your piece and you can restore their shine with a quick cleaning.

925 Silver Spacers

Organizers

Trays

These triangle-shape little trays are wonderful. They hold the beads in one place while you are beading and, when you are done, it is easy to return them to their containers with the funnel-like corner.

Bead Tray

Scoop

Rather than pick up scattered beads with your fingers, this scoop works a lot faster.

Boxes

Organize your findings and beads, you would know when you are running out, and you would know where to locate your items. To finish one project, you need your beads, clamshell bead tips, crimps, threading materials, jump rings, and clasp at the very least. The more organized you are the faster you finish your project and get to wear your new creation.

Tubes

These tubes let you see your colors and beads easily. It also saves space as you can have five or six compartments in one tube.

Ziploc and Cellophane Bags

Ziploc bags are good for keeping beads or necklaces together and are re-sealable. However, cellophane bags do a better job keeping the moisture out. Metal findings keep their shine longer when stored in a cellophane bag. Cellophane is a thin, transparent sheet made of regenerated cellulose. Its low permeability to air, oils, and grease maintains the beads' shine.

Chrome Plated Gem Scoop

Bead Tube

**Transparent
Box Organizer**

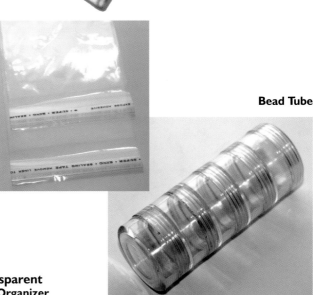

Opening and Closing a Jump Ring

Use any two pair of pliers to do this job. Similarly you can open or close the eye pin by using one hand to hold the pin and use a pair of pliers to open the loop by bringing the pliers towards you or away from you.

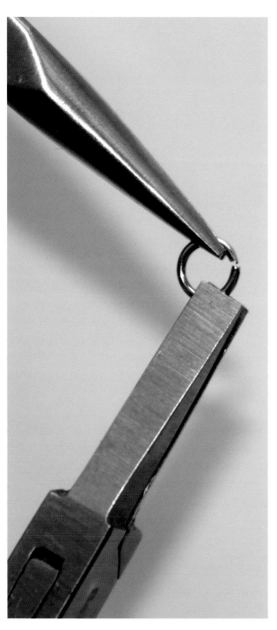

Hold the two sides of the jump ring with two pairs of pliers: flat-noise pliers and pointed-nose pliers.

Open the jump ring by pulling one pair of pliers towards you and the other pair away from you. Never try to open the jump ring by pulling the pliers apart sideways. Opening the jump ring apart sideways will weaken and deform the ring. Close the jump ring the same way.

Making a Simple Loop

This can be very useful for making chains and dangling earrings.

Use the cutter to cut the wire 0.39" (1cm) from the bend. You can measure the distance with your finger tip to save time.

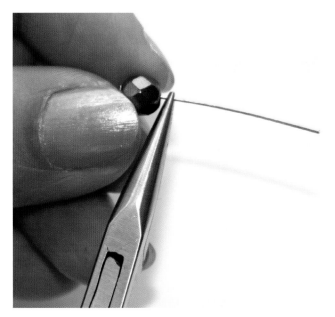

Hold the head pin and bead with your left hand.

Use the round-nose pliers to make the loop. If you need to thread this pin through leather or faux suede, you can make the loop a bit bigger.

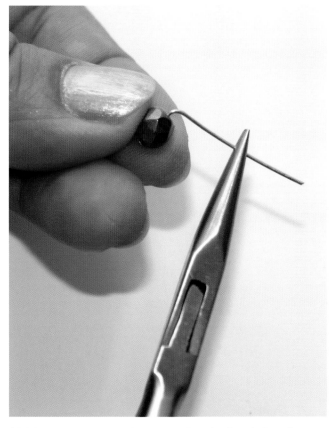

Hold the sharp-nose pliers near the pin. Bend the wire at a right angle.

Check the loop to make sure that it is straight and close.

Wrapping a Top Drilled Bead

Use this technique when you have a briolette.

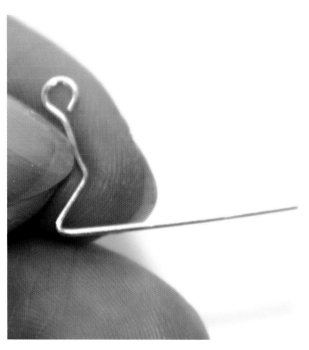

Using the sharp-nose pliers, bend the eye pin like this.

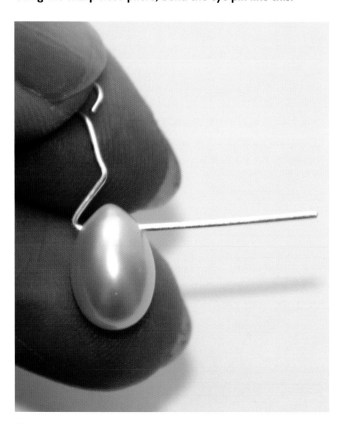

Place the top drilled bead in the pin.

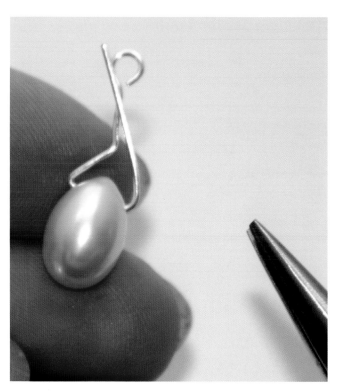

Use the sharp-nose pliers to bend the wire upwards to complete the triangle. The triangle will frame the bead nicely and the bead can move freely within the space.

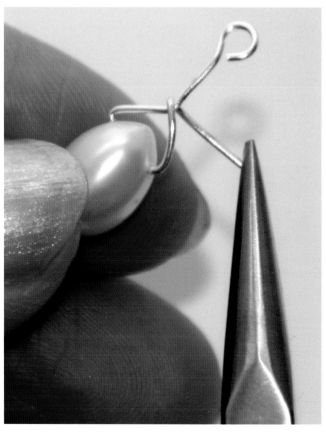

Wrap the tail around the base wire to form a little triangular hanger.

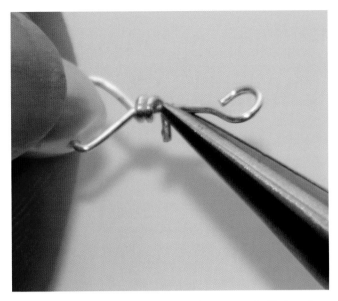

Turn the bead using your left hand; be sure to hold the pliers tight to keep the pin in place.

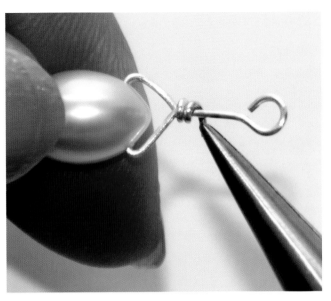

Wrap the end tightly and press the end down against the base wire.

This is the method to wrap a top-drilled bead. You can add a small bead or two on top of the drop bead to make it prettier as in the "It Rocks" project.

Single Strand Ending

There are different ways of ending a necklace or bracelet. Most of the projects in this book can end like this.

Thread the nylon through a clamshell bead tip. Slide a crimp bead onto the nylon. Flatten the crimp bead with a pair of sharp-nose pliers. Check to make sure that it is secured. Thread the nylon back through the clamshell bead tip and through a few beads. Tie a double knot (point A) thread through a few more beads and tie a single knot (point B). Hide the tail in the following beads. Trim off the excess. Close the clamshell. Join the hook of the clamshell bead tip to a jump ring and at the same time connect the jump ring to a clasp.

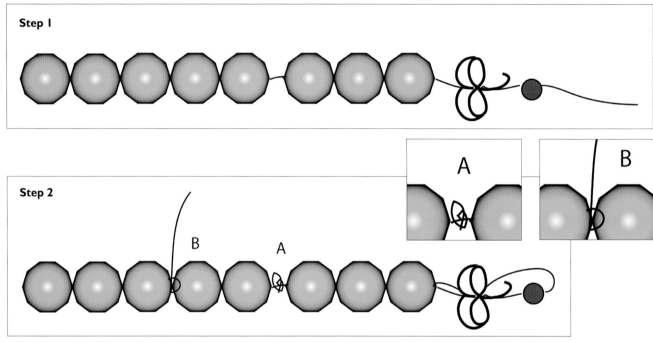

Step 1

Step 2

A

B

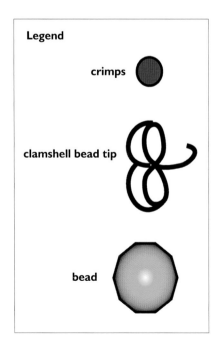

Legend

crimps

clamshell bead tip

bead

Multiple Strands Ending

Finish off each strand using the method above and then join the different strands together in a jump ring. Connect the jump ring to the clasp of your choice. You can hide the strands under the cover of bead caps or cones before attaching the clasp.

Using Spacers

When you have a weaved-necklace, there are two or more nylon strings to finish off. The beads are small and the hole size is tiny. It can be hard to put four thicknesses of nylon through the ending bead. In this case you can employ matching color spacers to finish off the necklace and hide the thread tails before joining the clasp.

Tension

As we know, tension in knitting is very important as it affects the look of the whole piece. Tension in beading is the same too. If the tension is too tight, the beads cannot sit comfortably and the flow is not smooth. This will affect the way that it sits or hangs. When the tension is too loose, you see the bare thread and that is not attractive at all.

Standards and Color Charts

I have enclosed in this chapter some helpful standards in table form for your reference. When making a creation of your own, a lot of questions will come to mind. The standards are great reference and they will guide you into making the best choices for your piece and save you time in the long run.

Standards

Common Ring Size Conversion Table

Inches (Inside Diameter)	Milimeters (Inside Diameter)	USA / Canada	British	Japan	Hong Kong	Switzerland
0.650	16.51	6	L½	12	13	12.75
0.666	16.92	6.5	M½	13	14.5	14.00
0.682	17.35	7	N½	14	16	15.25
0.698	17.75	7.5	O½	15	17	16.50
0.714	18.19	8	P½	16	18	17.75

Common Wire Size

Wire Diameter in Milimeters	American Wire Gauge
1.00	18
0.80	20
0.60	22
0.50	24
0.40	26
0.30	28
0.25	30
0.20	32

Common Jewelry Length

Type	Length
Bracelet	7" or 18cm (depending on the wearer — measure the wrist and add 0.6" or 1.5cm)
Ankle Bracelet	10" or 25.4cm
Choker	14-16" or 35.5 to 40.5 cm
Princess	18" or 45cm
Matinee	20-24" or 50-60cm
Eye Glass Holder	28" or 70cm
Opera	32" or 81cm
Rope	45" or 112.5cm
Lariat	48" or 122cm

Seed Bead

Common Seed Bead Size	# of Beads Per Inch (2.5cm)	# of Beads Per 1/16 oz (g)
14/0	26	256
11/0	20	100
8/0	12	48
6/0	10	17

Pearl Size

The size of pearls can be measured using a bead gauge.

Color Charts

As I mentioned before, color is the most important aspect of your creation. I have included two comprehensive color charts of SWAROVSKI® Elements. I have a few favorite colors and tend to limit myself to those color choices, but you can see here the variety and rich tone of color variations available. On top of this, SWAROVSKI® has different coatings called "Effect" added to the colors, so you would never be short on choices.

CREATE
YOUR STYLE
with SWAROVSKI ELEMENTS

beads, pendants

Numerical Order

001	Crystal	208	Siam	243	Capri Blue	362	Light Peach
001 AB	Crystal Aurore Boreale	209	Rose	246	Light Colorado Topaz	371	Violet
001 AB2	Crystal Aurore Boreale 2x	211	Light Sapphire	248	Sun	374	Indian Red
001 BBL	Crystal Bermuda Blue	212	Light Amethyst	249	Citrine	379	Indicolite
001 CAL	Crystal Comet Argent Light	213	Jonquil	267	Turquoise	383	Light Grey Opal
001 COP	Crystal Copper	214	Peridot	277	Purple Velvet	385	Lime
001 DOR2	Crystal Dorado 2x	215	Black Diamond	280	Jet	389	Violet Opal
001 GSHA	Crystal Golden Shadow	217	Indian Sapphire	280 HEM	Jet Hematite	390	Pacific Opal
001 HEL	Crystal Heliotrope	220	Smoked Topaz	280 HEM2	Jet Hematite 2x	391	Silk
001 MAT	Crystal Matt Finish*	221	Light Smoked Topaz	280 NUT2	Jet Nut 2x	393	Palace Green Opal
001 METBL2	Crystal Metallic Blue 2x	223	Light Rose	281	White Alabaster	394	Caribbean Blue Opal
001 MLG2	Crystal Metallic Light Gold 2x	225	Smoky Quartz	283	Provence Lavender	395	Rose Water Opal
001 MOL	Crystal Moonlight	226	Light Topaz	284	Greige	396	Dark Red Coral
001 REDM	Crystal Red Magma	227	Light Siam	285	Air Blue Opal	397	Mint Alabaster
001 SAT	Crystal Satin	228	Olivine	286	Mocca	398	Cyclamen Opal
001 SSHA	Crystal Silver Shade	229	Blue Zircon	287	Sand Opal	501	Ruby
001 VM	Crystal Vitrail Medium	234	White Opal	288	Dark Indigo	502	Fuchsia
202	Aquamarine	234 SBL	White Opal Sky Blue*	289	Indian Pink	508	Rosaline
203	Topaz	234 STS	White Opal Star Shine*	291	Fern Green	515	Burgundy
204	Amethyst	236	Hyacinth	293	Rose Alabaster	539	Tanzanite
205	Emerald	237	Fireopal	319	Vintage Rose	542	Padparadscha
206	Sapphire	238	Chrysolite	360	Erinite	550	Khaki
207	Montana	241	Garnet	361	Light Azore		

Alphabetical Order

Air Blue Opal (285)
Amethyst (204)
Aquamarine (202)
Black Diamond (215)
Blue Zircon (229)
Burgundy (515)
Capri Blue (243)
Caribbean Blue Opal (394)
Citrine (249)
Chrysolite (238)
Crystal (001)
Crystal Aurore Boreale (001 AB)
Crystal Aurore Boreale 2x (001 AB2)
Crystal Bermuda Blue (001 BBL)
Crystal Comet Argent Light (001 CAL)
Crystal Copper (001 COP)
Crystal Dorado 2x (001 DOR2)
Crystal Golden Shadow (001 GSHA)
Crystal Heliotrope (001 HEL)
Crystal Matt Finish* (001 MAT)
Crystal Metallic Blue 2x (001 METBL2)
Crystal Metallic Light Gold 2x (001 MLG2)
Crystal Moonlight (001 MOL)

Crystal Red Magma (001 REDM)
Crystal Satin (001 SAT)
Crystal Silver Shade (001 SSHA)
Crystal Vitrail Medium (001 VM)
Cyclamen Opal (398)
Dark Indigo (288)
Dark Red Coral (396)
Emerald (205)
Erinite (360)
Fern Green (291)
Fireopal (237)
Fuchsia (502)
Garnet (241)
Greige (284)
Hyacinth (236)
Indian Pink (289)
Indian Red (374)
Indian Sapphire (217)
Indicolite (379)
Jet (280)
Jet Hematite (280 HEM)
Jet Hematite 2x (280 HEM2)
Jet Nut 2x (280 NUT2)

Jonquil (213)
Khaki (550)
Light Amethyst (212)
Light Azore (361)
Light Colorado Topaz (246)
Light Grey Opal (383)
Light Peach (362)
Light Rose (223)
Light Sapphire (211)
Light Siam (227)
Light Smoked Topaz (221)
Light Topaz (226)
Lime (385)
Mint Alabaster (397)
Mocca (286)
Montana (207)
Olivine (228)
Pacific Opal (390)
Padparadscha (542)
Palace Green Opal (393)
Peridot (214)
Provence Lavender (283)
Purple Velvet (277)

Rosaline (508)
Rose (209)
Rose Alabaster (293)
Rose Water Opal (395)
Ruby (501)
Sand Opal (287)
Sapphire (206)
Siam (208)
Silk (391)
Smoked Topaz (220)
Smoky Quartz (225)
Sun (248)
Tanzanite (539)
Topaz (203)
Turquoise (267)
Vintage Rose (319)
Violet (371)
Violet Opal (389)
White Alabaster (281)
White Opal (234)
White Opal Sky Blue* (234 SBL)
White Opal Star Shine* (234 STS)

beads, pendants

Colours

  Crystal
001

 White Opal
234

 White Alabaster
281

 Rose Water Opal
395

 Rose Alabaster
293

 Rosaline
508

 Vintage Rose
319

 Light Rose
223

 Rose
209

 Indian Pink
289

 Fuchsia
502

 Ruby
501

 Padparadscha
542

 Sun
248

 Fireopal
237

 Hyacinth
236

 Indian Red
374

 Light Siam
227

Dark Red Coral
396

Siam
208

Garnet
241

Burgundy
515

Light Amethyst
212

  Violet Opal
389

 Violet
371

 Provence Lavender
283

 Tanzanite
539

 Cyclamen Opal
398

 Amethyst
204

 Purple Velvet
277

 Dark Indigo
288

 Montana
207

 Capri Blue
243

 Sapphire
206

 Light Sapphire
211

 Air Blue Opal
285

  Aquamarine
202

 Light Azore
361

 Indian Sapphire
217

 Pacific Opal
390

 Mint Alabaster
397

 Turquoise
267

Indicolite
379

Caribbean Blue Opal
394

Blue Zircon
229

Chrysolite
238

  Peridot
214

 Fern Green
291

 Erinite
360

 Emerald
205

 Palace Green Opal
393

 Olivine
228

 Khaki
550

 Lime
385

 Light Topaz
226

 Citrine
249

 Jonquil
213

 Silk
391

 Light Peach
362

 Sand Opal
287

 Light Colorado Topaz
246

 Topaz
203

Light Smoked Topaz
221

Smoked Topaz
220

Mocca
286

Smoky Quartz
225

Greige
284

Light Grey Opal
383

Black Diamond
215

Jet
280

Effects

 Crystal
Aurore Boreale
001 AB

 Crystal
Aurore Boreale 2x
001 AB2

 Crystal Satin
001 SAT

 Crystal Matt Finish*
001 MAT

 Crystal Moonlight
001 MOL

 Crystal Silver Shade
001 SSHA

 Crystal Golden Shadow
001 GSHA

 Crystal Copper
001 COP

 Crystal Red Magma
001 REDM

 Crystal
Comet Argent Light
001 CAL

 White Opal Sky Blue*
234 SBL

 White Opal Star Shine*
234 STS

 Crystal Bermuda Blue
001 BBL

 Crystal Heliotrope
001 HEL

 Crystal Metallic Blue 2x
001 METBL2

 Crystal Vitrail Medium
001 VM

 Crystal
Metallic Light Gold 2x
001 MLG2

 Crystal Dorado 2x
001 DOR2

Jet Nut 2x
280 NUT2

Jet Hematite
280 HEM

Jet Hematite 2x
280 HEM2

Classic Colours
Exclusive Colours

CRYSTAL *pearls*

Colours

 Crystal White Pearl
001 650

 Crystal Cream Pearl
001 620

 Crystal Creamrose Light Pearl
001 618

 Crystal Creamrose Pearl
001 621

 Crystal Gold Pearl
001 296

 Crystal Bright Gold Pearl
001 306

 Crystal Copper Pearl
001 159

 Crystal Coral Pearl
001 816

 Crystal Brown Pearl
001 815

 Crystal Deep Brown Pearl
001 414

 Crystal Bronze Pearl
001 295

 Crystal Peach Pearl
001 300

 Crystal Powder Almond Pearl
001 305

 Crystal Rosaline Pearl
001 294

 Crystal Powder Rose Pearl
001 352

 Crystal Lavender Pearl
001 524

 Crystal Mauve Pearl
001 160

 Crystal Burgundy Pearl
001 301

 Crystal Bordeaux Pearl
001 538

 Crystal Maroon Pearl
001 388

 Crystal Dark Purple Pearl
001 309

 Crystal Night Blue Pearl
001 818

 Crystal Light Blue Pearl
001 302

 Crystal Tahitian-look Pearl
001 297

 Crystal Powder Green Pearl
001 393

 Crystal Light Green Pearl
001 293

 Crystal Antique Brass Pearl
001 402

 Crystal Dark Green Pearl
001 814

 Crystal Platinum Pearl
001 459

 Crystal Light Grey Pearl
001 616

 Crystal Dark Grey Pearl
001 617

 Crystal Black Pearl
001 298

 Crystal Mystic Black Pearl
001 335

CRYSTAL *pearls*

Numerical Order

001 159	Crystal Copper Pearl
001 160	Crystal Mauve Pearl
001 293	Crystal Light Green Pearl
001 294	Crystal Rosaline Pearl
001 295	Crystal Bronze Pearl
001 296	Crystal Gold Pearl
001 297	Crystal Tahitian-look Pearl
001 298	Crystal Black Pearl
001 300	Crystal Peach Pearl
001 301	Crystal Burgundy Pearl
001 302	Crystal Light Blue Pearl
001 305	Crystal Powder Almond Pearl
001 306	Crystal Bright Gold Pearl
001 309	Crystal Dark Purple Pearl
001 335	Crystal Mystic Black Pearl
001 352	Crystal Powder Rose Pearl
001 388	Crystal Maroon Pearl
001 393	Crystal Powder Green Pearl
001 402	Crystal Antique Brass Pearl
001 414	Crystal Deep Brown Pearl
001 459	Crystal Platinum Pearl
001 524	Crystal Lavender Pearl
001 538	Crystal Bordeaux Pearl
001 616	Crystal Light Grey Pearl
001 617	Crystal Dark Grey Pearl
001 618	Crystal Creamrose Light Pearl
001 620	Crystal Cream Pearl
001 621	Crystal Creamrose Pearl
001 650	Crystal White Pearl
001 814	Crystal Dark Green Pearl
001 815	Crystal Brown Pearl
001 816	Crystal Coral Pearl
001 818	Crystal Night Blue Pearl

Alphabetical Order

Crystal Antique Brass Pearl (001 402)
Crystal Black Pearl (001 298)
Crystal Bordeaux Pearl (001 538)
Crystal Bright Gold Pearl (001 306)
Crystal Bronze Pearl (001 295)
Crystal Brown Pearl (001 815)
Crystal Burgundy Pearl (001 301)
Crystal Copper Pearl (001 159)
Crystal Coral Pearl (001 816)
Crystal Cream Pearl (001 620)
Crystal Creamrose Light Pearl (001 618)

Crystal Creamrose Pearl (001 621)
Crystal Dark Green Pearl (001 814)
Crystal Dark Grey Pearl (001 617)
Crystal Dark Purple Pearl (001 309)
Crystal Deep Brown Pearl (001 414)
Crystal Gold Pearl (001 296)
Crystal Lavender Pearl (001 524)
Crystal Light Blue Pearl (001 302)
Crystal Light Green Pearl (001 293)
Crystal Light Grey Pearl (001 616)
Crystal Maroon Pearl (001 388)

Crystal Mauve Pearl (001 160)
Crystal Mystic Black Pearl (001 335)
Crystal Night Blue Pearl (001 818)
Crystal Peach Pearl (001 300)
Crystal Platinum Pearl (001 459)
Crystal Powder Almond Pearl (001 305)
Crystal Powder Green Pearl (001 393)
Crystal Powder Rose Pearl (001 352)
Crystal Rosaline Pearl (001 294)
Crystal Tahitian-look Pearl (001 297)
Crystal White Pearl (001 650)

Classic Colours
Exclusive Colours

Cleaning Tips

Pearls

Keep pearls away from perfume and cosmetics to maintain their luster and shine. After each wear, wipe them thoroughly with a damp cloth and then air them out before storing.

Copper

Using diluted vinegar is very effective for cleaning copper.

Silver

I like to use a silver polish cloth to bring back the shine. You should never wash a silver polish cloth, as washing will get rid of the chemicals that came with the cloth. I had a bad experience with silver polish solution once. I soaked a silver chain in the solution and it came out broken. It also left ugly white residue on the hard-to-reach areas.

Gold

Use a gold polish cloth to polish. Alternatively, you can use a jewelry cleaning solution to maintain the shine.

Turquoise

Keep turquoise stones away from make-up, oil, perfume, and soap. They will fade under prolong sun exposure. Dry conditions may cause cracks and color change, so pamper and store your turquoise jewelry accordingly.

Metal

Metal findings and beads get tarnished easily. You do not have to throw them away. You can use Autosol® to clean them. Cleaners can be harsh, so always test with a small area first. Remember to wipe the metal with a clean cloth after the cleaning to remove any residual cleaner.

Glass/Crystal Beads

Soak them in soapy water overnight to clean. After a rinse the glass bead will restore its shine. Storing beads in Ziploc™ plastic bags. They keep dust and moisture away. Be careful with delicate beads — keep them stored separately so that they are not rubbed or crushed by other tougher materials.

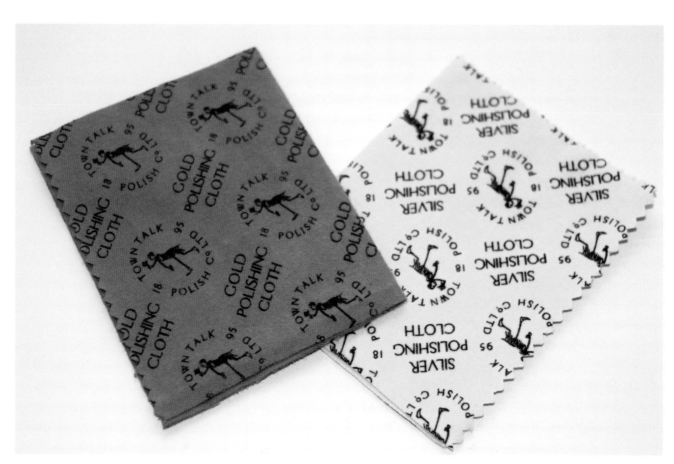

Gold and Silver polish cloths.

Inspirational
Gallery

Tango

Lady Chatterley

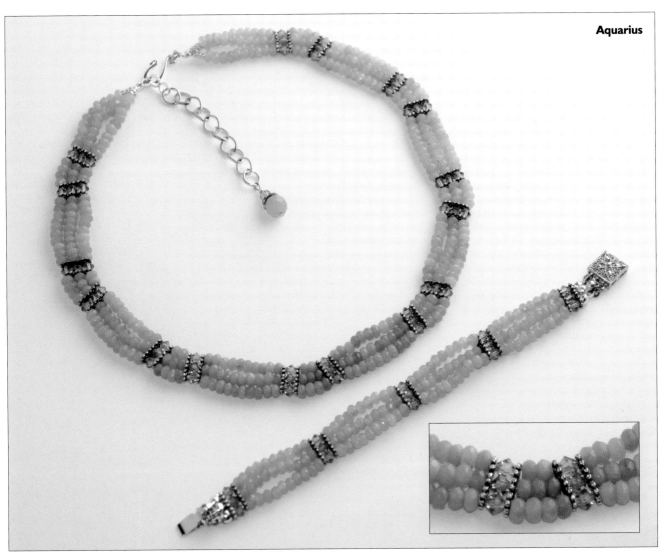

Aquarius

Cheery Berry

Amethyst Scent

Josephine

Temptation

Antique Green

Simplicity

Everyday Black

Brim

Scarlet

Moodi

Sunday Best

Tullie

Germaine

Tulip

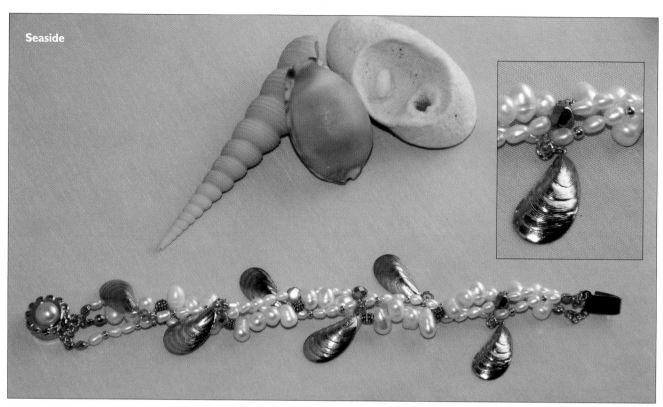

Seaside

Violet Romance

Robin

Big White

My Valentine

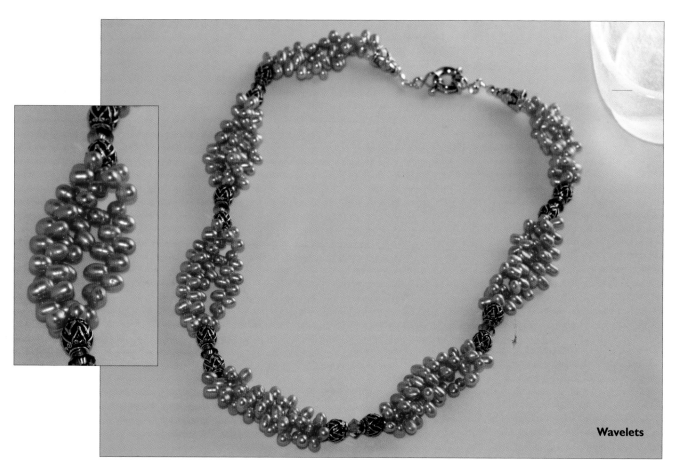

Wavelets

My Pumpkin